Challenging
Exceptionally Bright Children
in Early Childhood Classrooms

Also by Ann Gadzikowski
Story Dictation: A Guide for Early Childhood Professionals

CHALLENGING
Exceptionally **BRIGHT**
CHILDREN in Early
Childhood Classrooms

ANN GADZIKOWSKI

Foreword by Nancy B. Hertzog, PhD

Redleaf Press®
www.redleafpress.org
800-423-8309

Published by Redleaf Press
10 Yorkton Court
St. Paul, MN 55117
www.redleafpress.org

National Association for the
Education of Young Children
1313 L Street NW, Suite 500
Washington, DC 20005-4101
www.naeyc.org

First edition 2013
Cover design by Jim Handrigan
Cover photograph © Alloy Photography/Veer
Author photograph by David Linsell
Interior design by 4 Seasons Book Design/Michelle Cook
Typeset in Trade Gothic Lt Std and Janson Text
Interior photographs by Ann Gadzikowski except on page 111, by Aleksandra Muszynski
Printed in the United States of America
20 19 18 17 16 15 14 13   1 2 3 4 5 6 7 8

Excerpt from "Teaching Diversity: A Place to Begin" by Janet Gonzalez-Mena and Dora Pulido-Tobiassen was originally published in *Early Childhood Today* (November), © 1999 by Scholastic, Inc. Reprinted with permission of Scholastic, Inc.

Library of Congress Cataloging-in-Publication Data
Gadzikowski, Ann, author.
  Challenging exceptionally bright children in early childhood classrooms / Ann Gadzikowski.
  — First edition.
      pages cm
  Summary: "Challenging Exceptionally Bright Children in Early Childhood Classrooms will help you identify exceptionally bright children. It includes ideas to help you change the pace, level, or method of teaching in response to the needs of individual children and provides guidance for working with families" — Provided by publisher.
  Includes bibliographical references and index.
  ISBN 978-1-60554-116-7 (pbk.)
  ISBN 978-1-60554-252-2 (e-book)
  1. Gifted children—Education (Early childhood) 2. Gifted children—Education (Preschool)
I. Title.
  LC3993.218.G33 2013
  371.95—dc23
                        2012039059

Printed on acid-free paper

MIX
Paper from
responsible source
FSC® C011935

NAEYC Item #7217

To Alexa Jane,
my own exception

Contents

Foreword

Teaching young children is complicated. The most experienced and responsive teacher can be thrown off her game when a three-year-old asks how electricity works or what numbers are smaller than zero. This book, *Challenging Exceptionally Bright Children in Early Childhood Classrooms*, helps early childhood educators prepare for those moments in their day when a child's inquiry takes learning in a new direction. The author, Ann Gadzikowski, provides big ideas and essential understandings that will guide teachers to be responsive to unpredictable moments and students.

Gadzikowski threads three major ideas into every chapter of her book. These are the ingredients for challenging young children: differentiation, conversation, and connection. This book is filled with practical suggestions and numerous examples of how to challenge young children by connecting new learning experiences to what they already know, by paying attention to individual differences regardless of how gifted a particular group of children or an individual child may be, and by engaging children in conversations that scaffold their learning processes to provide authentic and meaningful learning experiences. Of particular value to the teachers who read this book are the rich and vividly described examples of actual teaching situations.

Gadzikowski recognizes the diversity in all early childhood classrooms and emphasizes the need for teachers to build upon children's interests and to treasure young children's misconceptions or mistakes as opportunities for deeper learning. She addresses with boldness the looming question in gifted education: Should young children who are cognitively and academically ahead of their age peers be separated from them? She responds to that question with substantiated research and literature that promotes the connection between cognitive, physical, social, and emotional growth. In chapter 6, she states, "Most young children will best benefit from a core classroom experience that is part of a general early childhood program serving a diverse population of learners" (59). Gadzikowski illuminates best practices of constructivism, where children learn from one another through hands-on, sensory experiences. This main idea is repeated again toward the end of the book in chapter 11, when she encourages parents to understand that "cognitive challenges for very young children are likely to involve hands-on projects and creative conversations, rather than worksheets and encyclopedias" (120).

All early childhood educators need to understand the foundations of early childhood education as well as have the expertise to challenge young children who have demonstrated atypically advanced development. Gadzikowski focuses on the strategies that equip teachers to provoke higher-level thinking in their students and to create environments that allow children to grow in their strength areas. In chapter 3, she encourages teachers to observe and document the behaviors and progress of their students and gives specific tips on how to listen, ask questions, and take meaningful notes on what the children are saying. These fairly simple ideas may be the difference between a teacher who knows and learns how to stimulate a child's thinking and a teacher who simply records what the child is doing without taking the opportunity to push the child further.

As a professor who teaches future early childhood educators, this book not only encompasses what we want them to know about teaching all young children but also gives practical suggestions for addressing individual needs, interests, and readiness levels for their diverse students. Many bright young children are advanced readers. In chapter 7, Gadzikowski provides a list of authentic opportunities for children to engage in advanced literacy, emphasizing the need to connect children's reading to their interests, not only their reading levels. She gives teachers strategies for differentiating math, literacy, and science and also explains how inquiry-based learning integrates core content into children's pursuits of their own questions. Gadzikowski details in chapter 9 what teachers need to do to guide children through the scientific method, including the small steps of writing down students' questions, eliciting predictions, and helping students find resources to answer their questions.

Throughout this book, Gadzikowski demonstrates that she knows young children and their parents well. She implores both parents and teachers to focus on children's interests, passions, and strengths and to not allow asynchronous development of young children to mask their unique talents, personality traits, or needs. She highlights the importance of relationships—adult to child and child to child—and gives justification for educators to provide warm, inclusive environments where "the diversity of all the children's strengths and talents is nurtured and supported, and collaborative learning occurs frequently" (61).

Finally, beyond a toolbox of strategies, Gadzikowski's book gives teachers ways of thinking about how to provide optimal challenge to their students, with the zone of proximal development in the forefront of their planning. By reading this book, teachers may acquire what they need to create the distinguished classroom espoused by Syliva G. Feinburg and Mary Mindess in their 1994 book, *Eliciting Children's Full Potential*: "The ability to challenge children intellectually is the critical ingredient that differentiates the ordinary classroom from the distinguished one" (83).

Nancy B. Hertzog, PhD
Professor of Educational Psychology
Director of the Robinson Center for Young Scholars
University of Washington

Acknowledgments

I'm very grateful to Susan Corwith and my colleagues at the Center for Talent Development at Northwestern University in Evanston, Illinois. Thank you for sharing your expertise with me. I'm also grateful to all the children I've worked with in the CTD Leapfrog program who have challenged and amazed me with their curiosity, creativity, and wit. Many thanks to editors Kyra Ostendorf and Emily Green for their knowledge, encouragement, and support; I'm grateful for your wise suggestions and editorial guidance.

Introduction

The Diversity of Learners

Grab a handful of pebbles along a shore. Open your hand and look at the mix of shapes and textures you've gathered. Among the dozens of small stones spread across your palm you will probably find one that is a bit smoother than the rest, another that is quite rough. Perhaps one pebble is a bit flatter than the others, another very round. The natural diversity of our world can be found everywhere you look, whether in the palm of your hand or in the classroom where you teach. Among every group of children you meet there will probably be one with a giddy sense of humor, one who is quiet and gentle, one who loves to sing, and so on. And in every early childhood classroom there is at least one exceptionally bright child, perhaps one whose unusual talents are easy to spot, or another who may need your support and encouragement before she is ready to share her gifts with the world.

The Exceptionally Bright Child

The exceptionally bright child may be the one who delights us with unusual questions (*If the world is spinning, why don't we all get dizzy?*) and surprises us with a sophisticated vocabulary (*The sand in the sandbox is really arid today*). The exceptionally bright child might also be the one who bites or hits for what seems like no reason, the one who uses classroom materials inappropriately (*I wanted to see what would happen if I glued the blocks together*), or the one who seems to live in his own dream world, never making a friend or even having a conversation with other children. The exceptionally bright child might also be the child who meticulously follows every school rule and carefully watches her teachers' faces for nonverbal clues about how to best please the adults in her life.

While the characteristics and behaviors of exceptionally bright children can vary widely, at the core these are the children with an unusual ability to focus on the tasks and topics that capture their interests. They are children with an advanced ability to use language, solve math problems, or understand science concepts, or children who are especially creative and seem to be able to make connections between ideas that are not obviously related. The term "exceptionally bright" also applies to children who have already mastered all or most of the learning outcomes of your standard curriculum or who have passed most of the developmental benchmarks well in advance of the target time line for their age. An exceptionally bright child might seem smart in

This illustration demonstrates the level of detail and complexity in the work of exceptionally bright young children.

a traditional academic sense, like the five-year-old who enjoys reading the dictionary. Teachers must also be open to the possibility that an exceptionally bright child might reveal his talents in surprising and unconventional ways. The child who is able to mimic his teachers with startling and unnerving accuracy or the one who spends an hour stacking buttons into careful piles, using a sorting system that only he seems to understand—these are also children with exceptional talents and abilities.

Meeting Their Full Potential

The purpose of this book is to guide teachers and caregivers in their efforts to challenge exceptionally bright children to help them reach their full potential.

Giving all children the chance to learn and achieve to the very best of their ability is a worthy mission for any early childhood program; it is our job to support the learning and development of every child, with an understanding that each child has different strengths and weaknesses and each child develops at a unique pace. Yet most of the time when we talk about a child's "potential" in early childhood education, we are most focused on the children who are falling behind, the ones who are struggling to meet even the most fundamental learning outcomes. It makes sense that we would pay close attention to these children and continually remind ourselves of their potential for success and achievement. But the opportunity to reach full potential is something every child deserves: every child who struggles and falls behind, every child who is doing just fine and meeting expectations, and every child who is exceptionally bright.

If the needs of exceptionally bright children are ignored when they are very young and just entering the academic world of learning, they may begin to believe that school is a dull place where they will receive very little attention from teachers. They may become bored or disengaged. The iconic motto "A mind is a terrible thing to waste" is just as true at the preschool level as at the college level. Imagine a child with musical talent who is never given a chance to sing or a child with athletic talent who is never allowed to run. Now imagine a child with an exceptional ability to think who is never asked a difficult question. Challenging exceptionally bright children gives them an opportunity to develop their talents and strengths, fulfilling their individual potential as well as opening doors for future academic and professional achievement.

The Braided Thread

This book emphasizes three broad strategies (see table 1.1) for meeting the needs of exceptionally bright children. The first strategy is *differentiation*. To differentiate means to change the pace, level, or method of teaching in response to the needs of individual children. The phrase "One size does *not* fit all" is often used in relation to differentiated instruction. You are probably already practicing differentiated instruction in your classroom in your everyday decisions about how you select materials and how you divide your attention among the children in your class. The strategies in this book will help you differentiate more intentionally, in your curriculum development, your instructional practices, and your learning environment, with an eye to making sure you are challenging all the children to meet their full potential.

The second strategy is *conversation*. As the Greek philosopher Socrates discovered more than two thousand years ago, one of the best ways to engage students in a learning process is through discussion. Even very young children can be engaged in conversations that challenge them to think deeply and creatively. Too often, when an exceptionally bright child surprises us with her knowledge or cognitive skill, our response is, "My, how smart you are!" The child might enjoy the praise, but at some point she needs a response that's going to help her continue to learn and grow. Conversational strategies for challenging exceptionally bright young children include asking questions and providing authentic feedback. Throughout the book I provide suggestions for how to give accurate and specific feedback, such as repeating the child's response in your own words and countering with an open-ended question that challenges the child to use higher-level thinking.

Finally, the third strategy is *connection*. Social learning theorists such as Lev Vygotsky (1978) have asserted that learning takes place within a social context. One of the most important functions of early childhood educators is to help children learn from each other. How we pair and group children, how we facilitate conversations and play, and how we model collaborative learning are all important strategies that are detailed in the following chapters. Understanding that we can enrich children's learning opportunities by helping them learn from each other will help you challenge exceptionally bright children within the context of a diverse learning community. Exceptionally bright children can play important roles in a learning community, actively participating in the learning process as collaborators, questioners, and leaders.

TABLE 1.1: The Three Strategies for Challenging Exceptionally Bright Young Children

Strategy	Structure	Definition	Example
Differentiation	Teacher to Class	Changing or adapting teaching practices, the curriculum, and/or the environment in response to the needs of individual children	Kira is a five-year-old who is already reading independently at a first-grade level. At naptime, when children are invited to choose a book to look at while on their cots, Kira's teacher makes sure the collection of books available in the book corner offers a variety of reading levels, including early readers and chapter books.
Conversation	Teacher to Child	Challenging a child to think more deeply, more creatively, or with more complexity through conversation or discussion	When Jeremy accurately estimates the number of pennies in a jar, his teacher replies, "Yes, that's right. Tell me how you figured it out. What strategies did you use?"

TABLE 1.1 (continued)

Strategy	Structure	Definition	Example
Connection	Child to Child	Intentionally creating and facilitating opportunities for children to learn from each other	Emma is fascinated by birds and is able to identify the species and breed of the birds she sees in the neighborhood around the school. Emma's teacher invites her to create a bird book and pairs Emma with Julianna for the project because Julianna loves to draw all kinds of animals.

These three strategies—differentiation, conversation, and connection—are like a braided thread that is woven throughout this book. Using any one of the strategies will benefit children, but when implemented in combination, this trio creates an especially rich and satisfying learning experience.

Overview of This Book

Chapters 1 and 2 of this book provide the foundation for understanding what it means to be exceptionally bright in an early childhood classroom. Chapter 1 describes the characteristics of exceptionally bright children in greater depth and offers an overview of the field of gifted education. Chapter 2 presents informal and formal assessment methods that can be helpful for identifying exceptionally bright children and describing their weaknesses and strengths.

Chapters 3 through 5 each focus on one of the three strategies for challenging exceptionally bright young children: differentiation, conversation, and connection. Chapter 3, on differentiation, offers suggestions for how to adapt the curriculum, teaching practices, and the learning environment to challenge exceptionally bright children while still balancing individual and group needs. Chapter 4 describes specific techniques for asking questions that promote complex and creative thinking and strategies for providing authentic feedback that will prompt children to think more deeply. Chapter 5 explains social learning theory and offers suggestions for grouping children and facilitating their interactions in order to increase opportunities for children to make connections and learn from each other.

The next three chapters focus on three specific curriculum areas: literacy (chapter 6), math (chapter 7), and science (chapter 8). Each of those discussions demonstrates how the three strategies from chapters 3 through 5 can be utilized in that curriculum area to challenge exceptionally bright children.

Chapter 9 focuses on an area of potential challenge for some exceptionally bright children: social-emotional development. This chapter is necessary because some exceptionally bright children struggle with forming and maintaining friendships.

The book concludes with one of the most important topics related to working with exceptionally bright children: how to work with their parents and families. Chapter 10 offers strategies for helping these families understand their children's gifts and struggles and for supporting families as they prepare to guide their children through their primary school years.

Opportunities for Growth

The strategies presented in this book will help early childhood teachers support and guide exceptionally bright children. The strategies of differentiation, conversation, and connection are absolutely essential to the development of exceptionally bright children, who require cognitive stimulation that challenges them to think with more complexity, depth, and creativity than their same-age peers. At the same time, these strategies will help create a richer learning environment for all children in the early childhood classroom.

If we do not take the time to develop specific plans and strategies to support and guide these advanced learners, the result will be, at best, a missed opportunity to nurture and engage a special talent and, at worst, the development of counterproductive behaviors that will continually disrupt the classroom environment. When the needs of exceptionally bright children are not recognized and their talents are not nurtured, they may become withdrawn, stubborn, and resistant. In fact, the young children who exhibit the most challenging behaviors in an early childhood classroom are often those most in need of a true cognitive challenge.

For some children, special talents are grown and developed over time, and we may not truly know a child's areas of strength until she is in elementary school or beyond. But sometimes a talent is demonstrated at a very young age. When exceptionally bright children are supported and challenged, the result is children who are confident about their abilities to think and learn, who are excited about school, and who make creative contributions to the classroom community.

Characteristics of Exceptionally Bright Children

Chapter 1

Every Classroom Is Diverse

Imagine you are the teacher of an early childhood classroom in which every child in the group is exceptionally bright. What topics or materials do you think the children would find most meaningful and engaging? How would you pace the curriculum? Even though every child in this imaginary classroom is exceptionally bright, it's difficult to answer these questions without getting to know the children first. The diversity of personalities, interests, behaviors, and learning styles among exceptionally bright children is just as varied as the diversity among all children.

Characteristics of Exceptionally Bright Young Children

Some exceptionally bright children are easy to spot. They may tell us directly, "I know that already!" Or they may demonstrate, through their actions and words, that they have knowledge and skills beyond those of most of the other children. For example, when you read a picture book about a rainy day and ask the class, "Where does rain come from?" One child shouts out, "From evaporation!" This is no doubt an exceptionally bright child who not only

7

demonstrates a sophisticated vocabulary but also shows that he knows about and is able to apply a complex concept, the water cycle, to the context of the picture book story.

But spotting the behaviors of exceptionally bright young children is not always so easy. In a typical early childhood classroom, where children do not yet participate in traditional academic activities such as writing reports, taking notes, solving equations, or taking tests, it may be hard to see that some children are demonstrating advanced cognitive skills and abilities. Also, sometimes these skills and abilities are difficult to recognize in children because those who are bored and needing a challenge may misbehave or use materials inappropriately. For example, a teacher invites the children to look at leaves and pinecones using the magnifying glasses at the science center. One child, Jane, eagerly approaches the table and spends ten minutes in quiet concentration studying the objects. However, a few minutes later, Jane is tapping the magnifying glass against the window, distracting other children and in danger of breaking both the magnifying glass and the windowpane. This may be the behavior of an exceptionally bright child who is indeed fascinated by science but needs guidance, conversation, and activities that will extend and deepen her experience at the science table and continue to challenge her to make new discoveries. Of course, not all exceptionally bright children misbehave when they are bored. Some are able to find appropriate outlets for their energy and curiosity and others simply withdraw.

There are a few specific behaviors and characteristics, however, that seem to be common among many exceptionally bright children. One is a long attention span, at least for the activities and topics that they are passionate about. For example, one day Jason spends forty-five minutes working alone with snap blocks, creating a chain of shapes that extends from one side of the room to another. It is important to keep in mind that for exceptionally bright children a long attention span is often born out of a passionate interest and insatiable curiosity, not the desire for friendship or to please a teacher and follow the rules. In Jason's case, the next day, when he is invited by a classmate to build with foam shapes in the block area, he may last for only five minutes before he's throwing blocks and spinning in circles. This inconsistency is characteristic of an exceptionally bright child whose focus of interest may be so specific and intense that only certain activities will capture his attention for long periods of time.

Another indicator that a child is exceptionally bright is a very good memory. An exceptionally bright child may be one who remembers, after a class baking project, the exact quantities of flour, cornmeal, sugar, and baking powder used to make the cornbread. Or she may be the one who reminds you that when the class visited a farm a year ago, the bus driver's name was Dan. An especially good memory may also play a role in the abilities of children with advanced language skills. An exceptionally bright child may remember words he has heard only once and use a very large and varied vocabulary in casual conversation. Young children with excellent memories and advanced verbal abilities may sound like little professors when they use sophisticated words like "evaporation" or "hypothesis."

Exceptionally bright children often demonstrate their cognitive abilities in the ways they make connections between ideas and things that are not, for most children, obviously connected. Consider the five-year-old who, when watching his baby brother learn to walk, says, "I know why babies wobble when they learn to walk. They're so small they can still feel the earth turning." Though his explanation is incorrect, this child has made an abstract and sophisticated connection between some scientific information he learned about the movement of the earth through space and his observation of his brother moving across his family's living room.

The enjoyment of very rich and complex pretend play may also be an indicator of exceptional abilities. For example, a child who is able to lead and orchestrate an intricate pretend-play scenario—such as the creation of a world in which ponies vie with bunnies for magical treats, including invisible ice cream—indicates an exceptional ability for abstract thought, as well as advanced language skills.

Children who are exceptionally bright sometimes struggle to make friends and respond appropriately to their peers. But occasionally the child's social interactions are the arena where a child's abstract thinking is best demonstrated. A child who is strongly empathic and understanding of other children's emotions, who displays unusually mature gestures of kindness to others, may do this because she is able to think abstractly, symbolically walking in someone else's shoes. The child who seems excessively concerned with fairness and justice, who seems unusually aware of the needs of others, may be able to do so because he has the cognitive ability to see issues and perspectives that most others do not.

Children Who Excel in One Specific Curriculum Area

Sometimes the children who are easiest to identify as exceptionally bright are those who demonstrate a clear interest and ability in one specific curriculum area, such as language, reading, math, or science. Perhaps you've met one of these children in your classroom:

The big talkers are children with advanced language abilities who always have something to say. They are keenly interested in a variety of subjects and will speak at great length about their areas of expertise. These children may be able to recall and recite long and complex songs, stories, or instructions, correctly using sophisticated phrases or idioms such as "stroke of luck" or "as a matter of fact." In addition to advanced vocabulary, big talkers are likely to use longer and more complex sentences, and show an interest in and ability to converse about more complex concepts. Big talkers often prefer talking with adults rather than with their peers because they feel only adults are able to understand them and respond to them in ways they find satisfying. Big talkers may also be able to do more with language than just use sophisticated words and converse about advanced subjects; they may also use language creatively, such as by making up their own words or language using a system of beeps and squeaks.

The early readers are children who can decode text independently and read with some fluency even before entering kindergarten. An example is a three-year-old child who can tackle beginning readers like *Go, Dog. Go!* by P. D. Eastman and is ready for something more challenging. Although she frequently chooses the book area during free-choice time, she often fidgets and seems bored during group time because the language and plots in the stories read to the class are not complex or challenging enough to hold her attention.

The little scientists are children who are insatiably curious about how things work. They'll take apart a tricycle rather than ride it. They may even deliberately bust open the old toaster you keep in the housekeeping area, just to see for themselves what it looks like inside. Or you might find a little scientist crawling on the floor under the bathroom sink because he's trying to figure out how the pipes carry hot and cold water to the faucets. Little scientists are probably keen observers, typically with very long and focused attention spans. They may spend every minute of outdoor play lying in the grass watching ants travel in and out of an anthill.

The puzzle experts are children with an early aptitude for math topics such as geometry. They see the world in shapes, lines, and angles. They can independently put together a hundred-piece puzzle and perhaps even explain their strategies as they do it. When they play with wooden or Lego blocks, they may not want to share with anyone because they already have such a clear vision for the structure they're going to build.

Asynchronous Development

It is important to understand that just because a child is advanced in one area, such as mathematical thinking, it doesn't mean the child will be advanced in other areas of development, such as verbal ability. Often children who have a special ability in one domain of development are developing normally in all other areas. An advanced ability in one area may indicate that this is an area of strength for this child in the future, a talent to be developed over time. Sometimes children with advanced development in one area are measurably delayed in another area. This unevenness may be seen in broad areas of development, such as in the child with advanced cognitive functioning who falls behind in fine-motor development or social skills. This may also be true within the domain of cognitive development; for example, a child with advanced verbal language skills may struggle to learn to recognize the letters in her name. Such uneven development is called "asynchronous development," and it is one of the reasons it is important to continually assess the progress of young children in our early childhood classrooms. We can't assume that if a child is growing in one area of development, the other areas are progressing at the same pace. This variation in a child's rate of progress across developmental domains is another reason we need to be prepared to differentiate, a topic that is discussed at length in chapter 3.

Square Peg in a Round Hole

As previously mentioned, though many are easy to spot, some exceptionally bright children may be difficult to identify, either because they have already learned to hide the ways they are different from other children or because their exceptional cognitive abilities cause them to think or behave in unusual ways. These children may frustrate us with their challenging behaviors, such as the defiant and aggressive child who takes all the puzzles apart and never helps put them back together again, or the passive and withdrawn child who sits at the window, intensely watching the construction workers digging a ditch instead of eating his snack. Bright children who are bored and lack cognitive challenges may simply refuse to participate in the tried-and-true, all-time favorite preschool activities teachers love to lead. They don't want to make applesauce out of apples in the fall. They don't want to make snowmen out of cotton balls in the winter. They may agree to plant flower seeds in the spring, but they'll insist on digging up the seeds every few days because they need to see exactly how the seeds are growing and changing.

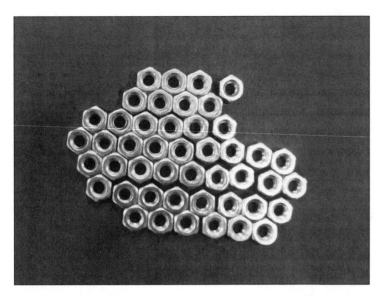
Exceptionally bright children sometimes prefer to use real materials rather than toys, and use them in unusual ways.

Not every child with challenging behaviors is an exceptionally bright child, but many are. When a child in your classroom is behaving in ways that frustrate or puzzle you, consider the possibility that this is an exceptionally bright child who is simply not challenged enough by a standard preschool or pre-K curriculum. She may have already mastered the lesson you stayed up late last night to prepare so carefully. Or she may learn so quickly that she understands in five minutes the concepts you intended to cover all week. Sometimes the exceptionally bright child in your class is not the big talker, the early reader, the puzzle master, or the little scientist. Sometimes the exceptionally bright child is the puzzling, quirky child who seems so hard to please.

Twice-Exceptional Children

The term "twice exceptional" is used in gifted education to describe children who are advanced academically or cognitively who have also been diagnosed with a disability or special need, such as attention deficit disorder (ADD) or Asperger's syndrome (AS). The needs of twice-exceptional children are complex because each one has a unique combination of strengths and weaknesses. The process of identifying a child as twice exceptional when the child's disability is a learning disorder such as dyslexia often does not happen until a child enters the primary grades and begins to have significant problems with schoolwork. The identification as twice exceptional is more likely to happen in early childhood if the child's disability is visible, such as with a physical disability or a disability that affects the child's social interactions like autism.

Autism and Asperger's Syndrome

Autism spectrum disorder (ASD) is a developmental disability that typically appears during the first three years of life and affects communication and social interactions. Autism is a "spectrum disorder" because there is a broad range of symptoms associated with it, from mild to moderate to severe. There is no known definitive cause of ASD, and for unknown reasons its diagnosis is on the rise in the United States. The Centers for Disease Control and Prevention (2012) has reported that one in eighty-eight children are identified with ASD.

According to the Autism Society (accessed 2012), the following are possible signs of autism in young children:

- lack of or delay in spoken language
- repetitive use of language and/or motor mannerisms (for example, flapping hands, twirling objects)
- little or no eye contact
- lack of interest in peer relationships
- lack of spontaneous or make-believe play
- persistent fixation on parts of objects

Asperger's syndrome (AS) is sometimes referred to as the mildest form of ASD. Children with AS often demonstrate good or even highly advanced language and cognitive skills, but they may be socially awkward and have trouble making eye contact. Children with AS often develop an interest in a specific topic, such as baseball or bridges, and memorize surprisingly large numbers of facts about this area of interest.

Some children who are exceptionally bright, especially those who show a strong and intense fascination with a single topic, might also demonstrate behaviors that are similar to the symptoms of AS and ASD. Only a trained professional such as a developmental pediatrician or a pediatric neurologist is qualified to make a diagnosis of AS or ASD. As early childhood professionals, we must exercise extreme caution and sensitivity in how we talk to children's families about what we are observing in the classroom. We must take care to describe only what we see and never hint or suggest to families that AS or ASD might be a possible diagnosis. Our role is to encourage family members to seek additional consultation, screening, and evaluation.

Exceptionally bright children with ASD or AS, or those who have symptoms and behaviors that are similar to children with ASD or AS, may present unique challenges in the early childhood classroom environment. Many treatments and responses have been shown to be effective in helping individuals with ASD and AS function successfully in the classroom. For example, for children with an intense interest in a specific topic, the interest can be used as a starting point for further learning. There is no reason to steer children away from topics that they find fascinating. For example, a child's interest in horses can be used to encourage that child to learn more about how large-animal veterinarians care for horses. If the child is having trouble joining in social play with other children, that child could be encouraged to pretend to be a horse on the playground with other children.

But Are They "Gifted"?

Children who seem advanced in cognitive development may be described in a variety of ways. Family members and teachers might use words like "bright" or "smart." In casual conversation, we might use words like "brainy" or even "quirky." However, the question arises whether it is appropriate to use more formal terms or phrases, for instance, "gifted" or "academically talented" or even "genius" or "prodigy," which tend to be used when describing older, school-age children.

A look at the literature on the subject of gifted education shows that educators and researchers rarely agree on a single definition of giftedness. Some prefer to use the term "talented" to generally describe a child with significant academic strengths who performs well in school. Others may use only specific criteria, such as intelligence tests, to define exactly which students are considered gifted (Olszewski-Kubilius, Limburg-Weber, and Pfeiffer 2003).

In early childhood education, most practitioners would agree that children five and under are too young to receive the label "gifted." During these early years, children are growing and developing so rapidly that it's just too soon to make predictions, either positive or negative, about a child's future academic performance. When speaking with families about their children's growth and progress, I recommend caution in using premature labels such as "gifted." It's far more important that we communicate to families that we know their children well, we recognize their talents and strengths, and we are prepared and willing to support and challenge their children to help them meet their full potential.

Another reason why the term "gifted" is rarely used in the early childhood field is that practitioners are sensitive to the idea that intelligence, as we tend to define it in the United States, is a cultural construct based on test taking, pencil-and-paper tasks, and learning to read, add, and fill in the blank. These things are too often thought of as the primary measures of what it means to be smart.

Multiple Intelligences

There are many educators, psychologists, and researchers, especially in the field of early childhood education, who recognize that there are multiple ways to define intelligence. One of the best-known proponents of this view is Howard Gardner, a developmental psychologist who created the theory of multiple intelligences. Gardner proposes that what we might call "book smart" is just one kind of intelligence. He suggests there may actually be at least eight different kinds of intelligence (Gardner 1999, 2006):

1. **Verbal/linguistic** describes young children who might be especially talented in reading, speaking, and singing. They might be able to memorize the words to a complicated song after just one listen and then perform the song by heart, as well as adapt the song by changing the words to make their own versions.

2. **Logical/mathematical** describes young children who are able to think conceptually, use clear reasoning, and recognize abstract relationships. They might be able to create a steering system for a wagon on their own by observing the relationships between the movement of the handle, the turning of the wheels, and the direction of travel.

3. **Visual/spatial** describes young children who see the world in colors and shapes. They might be able to complete a complex puzzle, create a patterned mosaic using colored blocks, or draw a road map of their neighborhood showing landmarks such as their home and school.

4. **Bodily/kinesthetic** describes young children who use bodily sensations, like touch, to learn about the world. They might be children who fidget all through story time but then create a graceful and expressive dance that retells the fairy tale they just heard.

5. **Musical** describes young children who learn through rhythm and melody. They might learn to play a musical instrument with relative ease and, in school, use sounds to help themselves learn and remember important facts and ideas.

6. **Interpersonal** describes young children who are very social. They understand and care about people. They learn best in a group and enjoy having a partner for most activities.

7. **Intrapersonal** describes young children who are unusually self-directed. They need at least a little quiet time alone every day.

8. **Naturalist** describes young children who are insatiably curious about science and nature. They enjoy being outdoors and keenly observe the changes in the weather, the growth of plants, and other natural phenomena.

If we limit our expectations of what it means to be smart to stereotypic "bookish" behaviors like reading and using multisyllabic words, we might miss the opportunity to recognize all these different types of intelligence. At the same time, while every child has at least one of these strengths, exceptionally bright children have exceptional strengths that go above and beyond those of the average child, especially in the areas related to cognitive development, such as verbal/linguistic, logical/mathematical, and naturalist. The information and strategies in this book are especially focused on these types of intelligence and will help you support children who have unusual strengths in these areas, especially those who are not challenged by the current curriculum offered in their classrooms.

Assessment and Identification of Exceptionally Bright Children

Measuring Potential

Think about the children in your current classroom. Are there any you suspect might be exceptionally bright? How do teachers and families know if a child is exceptionally bright? As described in chapter 1, some children's talents are more obvious, whereas other children's talents are difficult to identify. We might have a hunch, a gut instinct we've refined over years of working with children. Or we might have a guess based on a specific interaction or experience with a child. To effectively plan an engaging and challenging curriculum, however, you need more than a guess or a hunch. You need specific information about what each child can and cannot do now and what she or he might be able to achieve in the future.

Individual assessment of a child will give us useful information about how to support learning and help that child develop. There are usually three primary sources of assessment information:

- observable behaviors in the classroom
- conversations with families
- formal screening and evaluation tools

The assessment process will be most meaningful and helpful if it employs all three sources, because each has its unique strengths. The documentation of a child's observable behaviors provides valuable information about a child's learning experience at school. Information from families has to be part of this equation because in most cases no one knows a child better than his or her own family. And formal screening and evaluation tools provide specific information about how the child is developing relative to other children of the same age.

The purpose of identifying exceptionally bright children isn't to give them an early advantage. In early childhood, extra points are not awarded for being bright. The idea here is to get to know a child as well as we possibly can so we can best support the child's learning and growth. A quick mind and a curious nature are just starting points, not the endgame. The goal of assessment should be to gather information we can use to support the child in reaching his or her full potential.

What to Look For

The Frances A. Karnes Center for Gifted Studies at the University of Southern Mississippi (n.d.) is one of the few gifted education programs that has conducted research and created literature specific to early childhood. The center uses the term "gifted" in its literature, even though as I've mentioned it is a term applied mainly to children in the primary and secondary grades. Terminology aside, researchers at the Karnes Center have identified a set of cognitive characteristics and social/emotional characteristics that are unique to very young exceptionally bright children and that can serve as a helpful framework for early childhood educators.

The cognitive characteristics of exceptionally bright children include the following:

- early language development
- advanced vocabulary
- interest in symbols and the alphabet
- intense curiosity
- sustained attention
- generation of original ideas
- excellent memory
- creative/imaginative capacity

The social/emotional characteristics of exceptionally bright children include the following:

- emotional intensity/sensitivity
- frustration with own limitations
- concern with truth and fair play
- mature sense of humor
- perfectionism

The Power of Observation

The first and best tool for assessing a child's strengths is observation. All kinds of observation tools exist out there, from checklists to elaborate forms. It often is helpful to use a development checklist to measure the milestones that the child has already been able to reach. But because exceptionally bright children are just that, exceptional, at some point you will probably have to set aside the prescribed tool and take anecdotal notes about what you observe.

Anecdotal notes should include specific descriptions of a child's actions and behaviors, especially when a child chooses to use materials in a novel way, such as using paper, scissors, and tape to construct a miniature lawn mower. Note the date and the amount of time the child spends engaged in the task. Anecdotal notes may also include transcriptions of a child's conversations, questions, and explanations. For example, when a child is solving a difficult jigsaw puzzle, her exceptional ability to solve the puzzle may be demonstrated by the complexity of the puzzle itself as well as by her description of the problem-solving strategies she uses: "I started with the corners because I knew there were only four of them."

Listening to Children

While the term "observation" typically suggests using our eyes to watch, an especially essential component of observation is listening. A teacher's ears are just as important as her eyes for collecting information about children. In chapter 4, I discuss the importance of listening as a critical component in having meaningful and stimulating conversations with children. In that context I offer some general pointers for practicing effective listening. But listening is also critical for specifically assessing children's learning and development.

Experienced early childhood professionals have come to expect a certain level and type of response from children in various classroom situations. Yet exceptionally bright children often surprise us. Being open to those surprises and getting to know an exceptionally bright child through observation and listening require us to set aside preconceived notions of what are developmentally appropriate expectations for preschool and pre-K children. Here are two strategies to utilize in listening to exceptionally bright children for the purpose of assessing them.

1. **Restate.** When you're sure the child has finished talking, restate what the child has said. Summarize and ask follow-up questions. If you are questioning a child to assess what she knows about the weather, you might ask, "Where does rain come from?" If the child responds, "The water from the sea gets hot and turns into clouds," you could restate what the child says, perhaps tweaking it slightly to try to verify what the child understands about evaporation, and then ask a follow-up question. (*Hmm. The heat makes the water from the sea turn into clouds? How does the heat change the water?*)

2. **Take notes.** Write down what the child has said, word for word, so you can refer to it later. Explain to the child what you're doing. (*What you're saying is important. I'm writing it down because I want to remember what you said.*)

> According to Abby
>
> When asked "Where does rain come from?" Abby replied: "The water from the sea gets hot and turns into clouds. The heat makes the water foggy. After a while, there's so much water in the clouds that the clouds can't hold on to the water anymore and the water falls down in drops and that's rain. It's like the cloud has to go pee!"

The Family's Perspective

No assessment would be complete without the family's perspective. Regardless of how many hours the child spends in preschool or child care, most often no one knows the children you teach better than their families. The best way to gather information from family members is not at all revolutionary: Ask them!

While most families are at some point delighted by the clever and funny comments and behaviors of their children, most are also surprisingly accurate in their ability to identify when their children are advanced compared to other children of the same age. In fact, the families with the most accurate understanding of their children's advanced cognitive skills are often the ones who are anxious rather than pleased. This is because they have the awareness that their children are "different" from other children in a significant way, and they may already be questioning whether a traditional school environment can meet the needs of their children.

Some of the questions you might ask family members of a child who seems exceptionally bright include these:

- What activities does your child most enjoy at home?
- What are your child's interests? How intense is this interest? How much energy and enthusiasm does your child show for these topics of interest?
- What does your child seem curious about? What questions does your child ask?
- What surprises you about your child?
- Does your child have a good memory? If so, what does your child tend to remember most easily?
- What books, movies, or shows does your child enjoy?
- How long is your child's attention span for the activities that interest him or her?
- Does your child have a special interest in solving problems?
- Does your child have a special interest in clocks, calendars, maps, or money?
- Does your child have a vivid imagination? How do you know?
- Does your child enjoy drawing or writing? Can you show me some examples of what he or she draws or writes at home?
- Does your child enjoy playing games? What kinds of games does he or she enjoy most?
- Does your child use a computer? If so, how does he or she use it?
- Does your child like to be outdoors? What does your child enjoy doing outdoors?
- Does your child have a good sense of humor? What does he or she find funny?

The responses you receive to these questions may affirm what you already know and have observed about the child. Or they may fill some gaps in your understanding of the child and give you some insights on how to better engage the child in the life of the classroom or give you ideas about how to start and develop conversations with the child or find common interests between this child and other children in the group. At the same time, listening to and affirming families' descriptions of their children helps support and encourage them. Your feedback will show that you see and respect their child's uniqueness. This may be especially important if the family is concerned about their child's development and friendships.

Formal Screening and Evaluation

If you and the family agree that there is reason to believe the child might be exceptionally bright, the next step may be a formal screening and/or evaluation. Federal law guarantees free screening for developmental delays or disabilities by public school districts, but the ease of accessibility and the format of the screening can vary quite a bit from district to district. An initial screening is a general measurement of fine- and gross-motor development, vocabulary and speech development, and social-emotional growth. Many screening tools also measure indicators of general school readiness, for example, the identification of shapes and colors. There are two reasons for conducting a screening: One is to gather a very general description of a child's developmental strengths and weaknesses. The second reason is to check for indications of developmental delays or disabilities. The screening results may indicate that a child is ahead or behind in one or more areas of development. If that is the case, the next step may be a full developmental evaluation from the school district or a private educational psychologist.

A variety of formal evaluation tools are available. These are one-on-one tests conducted by a trained tester, often a psychologist, who asks the child to perform certain tasks, such as putting together a wooden puzzle or answering a series of questions. Two of the most commonly administered early childhood evaluation tools are the Wechsler tests and the Kaufman Assessment Battery (Washington State OSPI 2008).

The family of Wechsler tests include the Wechsler Preschool and Primary Scale of Intelligence (WPPSI), designed to evaluate children between the ages of two and seven years old. The Wechsler tests focus solely on cognitive development, providing scores in the areas of verbal comprehension, perceptual reasoning, working memory, and processing speed. The Kaufman battery is another evaluation tool used to measure intelligence. When administered to young children, it often includes two tests, the Kaufman Brief Intelligence Test (KBIT) and the Kaufman Test of Educational Achievement (KTEA). The final scores for both the Wechsler tests and the Kaufman tests are nationally normed, which means their scores are in the form of percentages that indicate how the child performed compared to other children of the same age who also took the test. So, for example, a verbal comprehension score of 95 percent means that the child is in the top 5 percent of children across the nation in the ability to comprehend verbally. Some enrichment programs for young children, such as summer programs for gifted or academically talented students, will require these kinds of tests to determine eligibility.

Remember, don't be surprised if a child who is advanced in one area of development is also delayed in another area. Explaining this concept of asynchronous development to parents may be helpful (see chapter 1). Sometimes families have unreasonable expectations of a very bright child because one area of the child's growth is so far ahead of other children's. They may expect the child to be advanced in every area. Reassure families that it would be most unusual for a child to excel in all areas of development.

Ongoing Assessment

The preschool years are a time of rapid growth and development for all children. For exceptionally bright children who remember, learn, and master new concepts quickly, it can be hard for us to keep track of their new milestones and accomplishments. An ongoing system of collecting portfolio documentation or work sampling is the easiest and most accurate way to monitor growth and development over an extended period of time.

"Portfolio documentation" is a broad term that can apply to any collection of classroom artifacts, including photos, work samples, dictated stories, or anecdotal notes, that can be used to document or measure children's growth and progress. Many curricula and assessment systems, such as the widely used Teaching Strategies Gold, include a portfolio component.

The Work Sampling System (WSS), as developed by a team led by Dr. Sam Meisels, involves collecting documentation of children's learning from multiple sources to evaluate what children know and can do. The WSS also includes a developmental checklist.

Dictation and Drawings as Assessment Tools

The use of dictation and drawings for ongoing assessment is of special note because both methods can be particularly helpful in representing the knowledge, interests, and growth of exceptionally bright children. The term "dictation" refers to any time an adult or older child writes down or transcribes the spoken words of a young child. Dictation can be helpful in documenting a child's knowledge in a specific area, for example, writing down a child's description of how the plumbing of a house works (*The pipes hold the water and the water pushes up through the walls into the sink upstairs*). The dictation of original stories gives us a glimpse inside a child's creative imagination. Dictated stories also demonstrate a child's vocabulary and understanding of narrative structure. The following story is from a four-year-old child. This example shows how young children who are still learning grammar and syntax have the potential to create very imaginative and complex stories.

> Once there is castle has everything. Even nine princesses and nine dogs. When winter comes the boy came and hurt the princess in the night except the princess is magic and doesn't get hurt. And then two robbers coming take two princesses home and tied them up. The next night is good-guy prince but he is lost and the magic princess find him and marries him inside her castle because it is so beautiful. But then the bad king came and stole the magic princess but she is not afraid. The king is magic but she makes him unmagic so he can't use his magic. She makes him into a frog and makes herself into a magic shark and she ate up his castle. Then the good-guy prince comes back and she makes him magic too so he is never afraid forever.

For children with on-level or advanced fine-motor skills, drawings can also represent what they know. Educators inspired by the Reggio Emilia schools in Italy have championed the use of drawings to document and reflect upon the learning process. For example, American educator George Forman demonstrated this Reggio Emilia–inspired teaching practice in the video *Jed Draws His Bicycle* (Videatives 2006). When children are asked to draw what they know or notice about a specific topic, such as bicycles or animals, the drawing process guides them toward observing and reflecting in ways that are different from what happens during a conversation. When children are asked to represent what they know in more than one way, such as with both words and pictures, or with both blocks and drawings, learning deepens.

This drawing by a four-year-old shows the child's ability to document detailed characteristics of animals.

Dictation and drawings both capture learning, for assessment, and provide an opportunity for conversation and reflection, which stimulates additional learning. Dictation and drawings also offer clues about what interests and excites children, which can help guide curriculum planning.

The Role of Pre-Assessment in Curriculum Planning

There is one more category of assessment that is particularly important in meeting the needs of exceptionally bright young children: the practice of pre-assessment. Before we begin teaching a new concept, skill, or unit, we need to find out what children already know. It seems reasonable and logical that we would not want to waste our time teaching children something they already know. Yet, in my experience, the concept of pre-assessment is rarely discussed among early childhood teachers. The children are so young that we often assume they have no prior knowledge or experience with the concepts we introduce in our curriculum. But for children who are exceptionally bright, who learn quickly and who have advanced knowledge on a variety of topics, we may be surprised to discover that they already know a great deal of the standard preschool or pre-K curriculum.

One of the ways to pre-assess—to find out what children already know about a topic—is to simply ask them. If you are about to begin a unit on airplanes, you could initiate a conversation at the snack table (*Who knows something about airplanes?*). A series of open-ended questions about airplanes (*What makes airplanes fly? How are airplanes different from boats?*) may elicit valuable information about prior knowledge children have about the topic.

Another way to gather pre-assessment information is by observing children engaged in a task or in play. The process of watching and listening to children play with toy airplanes may reveal prior knowledge children have about the topic. Pretend play about going on an airplane ride would be a similar source of good information.

Parents and family members are another source of pre-assessment information. For example, you might ask, "Has your child ever been on an airplane before? Does she seem curious about how airplanes work?" These pre-assessment activities improve your teaching and increase the children's engagement and interest because you are then better able to tailor the curriculum unit to children according to their abilities and interests.

Differentiation: Adapting the Curriculum, Teaching Practices, and the Learning Environment

Chapter 3

Defining Differentiation

Challenging exceptionally bright children in a general preschool or pre-K classroom requires differentiation. To differentiate means to adjust or change to meet the individual needs of each child. You can differentiate the way you develop the curriculum, the way you teach, and the way you organize the classroom environment. The term differentiation is frequently used in the field of gifted education as a primary strategy for challenging academically advanced students in a regular classroom. For example, a second grader who is able to read at an eighth-grade level may be given a more advanced reading assignment than the other second-grade students.

In early childhood education, the term differentiation is used less frequently. This may be because we early childhood educators more than likely have a background in child development, and we already approach our work with the assumption that teachers must make adjustments for the individual needs and varied developmental stages of each child. We know that development from birth through age five occurs so rapidly and in several different arenas at once: cognitive and language development, small- and large-motor development, and social-emotional development. And we have firsthand knowledge that each child is learning and growing at a unique pace. With this understanding of child development, the individualizing of our interactions with children, in accordance with their abilities, temperaments, and interests, is so fundamental it hardly needs a label. We individualize every day, especially in the caregiving, the conversations, and the social interactions we have with children, from helping them put on their shoes to serving them snacks.

While early childhood professionals usually do not need to be convinced that differentiation is important in caregiving tasks, we do tend to need support in incorporating differentiation strategies into curriculum planning, instructional strategies, and preparing the learning environment. For example, creating one single curriculum plan for the whole class is common practice among preschool and pre-K teachers. These plans are usually not differentiated or they may only be differentiated to meet the needs of the children who are struggling, not the children who are advanced and have already met the goals of the lesson.

Differentiation in Action

Here I present possible differentiation strategies used in gifted education and discuss how these strategies might be used in an early childhood classroom, using the example of one pair of pre-K teachers, Claire and Beth, and their experience teaching a unit on pets to their class. The strategies they implement for differentiation can be divided into three categories:

- strategies for differentiating the curriculum
- strategies for differentiating teaching practices
- strategies for differentiating the learning environment

As Claire and Beth begin planning their curriculum unit on the topic of pets, they have identified two learning objectives for the unit that are aligned with their program's mandated early learning standards: Children will observe and describe characteristics and needs of pets; and children will demonstrate, through play, how people take care of pets. Claire and Beth are aware that two children in the class—Maria and Nathan—have already mastered these objectives.

Maria is exceptionally bright. She is a very verbal child who seems to have a lot of advanced knowledge in a variety of topics. She is beginning to read on her own and has a very sharp memory for the language of stories. One of her favorite books is *Doctor De Soto* by William Steig, the story of a mouse who is a dentist. Claire and Beth have observed and noted that Maria is able to retell the entire story using a hybrid combination of decoding words and remembering. They have also had conversations with Maria about the content of *Doctor De Soto*. Their combined observations and conversations have led Maria's teachers to be aware of her extensive prior knowledge of animals and pets and how to care for them.

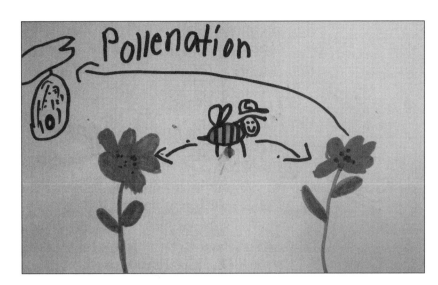

An exceptionally bright five-year-old represents a growing understanding of pollination.

Nathan's father is a veterinarian, and their family has two cats and three dogs at home. Nathan has already learned a lot about pets because of his experience in his family. Although he is not necessarily exceptionally bright, he does have extensive knowledge on this particular topic.

Strategies for Differentiating the Curriculum

When considering how to differentiate the curriculum, it's important to remember that, above all, the curriculum must be meaningful to young children. Most children are motivated to learn when their learning is connected to their real lives. This is true for exceptionally bright young children, too. The richest learning takes place when children can make meaningful connections between the new information and ideas they are learning and the experiences and knowledge that are already familiar and important to them.

This means that when we set out to differentiate the curriculum and look for ways to challenge exceptionally bright children, we can use their prior knowledge, experience, and interests as starting points and build from there. So, as one example, we can assume that Nathan, the child whose father is a veterinarian, has a great deal of prior knowledge about pets. This curriculum topic will certainly be very meaningful to him. Once the unit is under way and the children have begun developing questions about animals and how to take care of them, Nathan could be asked to deliver the class's questions to his father for help in answering them. His father could also be invited to visit the classroom. By giving Nathan the role of asking for his father's help with the class's research, the teachers are making a connection with what Nathan already knows is important to him. They are also creating opportunities for Nathan, and for all the children who have met Nathan's father, to learn about animal care in a meaningful context.

Use an Inquiry Process

One of the most powerful ways to challenge children to think is to encourage them to ask their own questions and to seek their own answers. The questions children ask can then be used to develop and differentiate the curriculum. This may mean intentionally withholding information from children in order to give them the opportunity to figure out something on their own.

We may already be doing this in small or large ways. Here's an example of a small, spontaneous inquiry process. A child asks her teacher, "Do we need to wear our boots on the playground today?"

The teacher directs the child to look out the window. "What do you see?" asks the teacher.

"I see a little bit of snow on the grass," replies the child.

"Ah, so there's snow on the grass," says the teacher. "Well, do you think we should wear boots today?"

"Yes," replies the child. "We need to wear our boots. Because there's some snow."

The same kind of inquiry process can be used for answering deeper and more complex questions. Children's big questions can be used to shape the curriculum and the decisions we make about what to teach and when to teach it. In the case of Beth and Claire's pet unit, suppose Nathan, the child whose father is a veterinarian, is playing pet hospital in the dramatic play area and a child brings a toy horse to the hospital. Nathan says, "First we have to weigh him." He puts the toy horse on the scale and comments, "If this was a real horse, he wouldn't fit on this scale."

Beth, observing the play, makes a note of Nathan's comment. Later, she talks with Nathan about what she observed, saying, "You were right about real horses. They're too big to fit on such a small scale."

Nathan asks Beth, "How do animal doctors know how much horses weigh?"

"That's a great question," says Beth. Then she gives the question back to Nathan and challenges him to seek his own answers. "That's such an interesting question, I'm going to write it down." She writes down Nathan's question and tapes it up on the wall of the classroom. "Nathan, how are we going to find out the answer to your question?"

"We could ask my dad," says Nathan.

"That's a good idea," says Beth. "Let's do that. What are some other ways we could find out?"

Beth helps Nathan make a list of possible strategies that include "looking in a book," "calling someone who has a horse," "going to a store that sells really big scales," and "visiting a horse farm." As Beth and Nathan work on this list, several other children become interested in Nathan's inquiry. Nathan's question becomes a small project that involves a group of children over the course of several weeks.

These conversations could lead to an emergent curriculum unit or to a small-group investigation concerning concepts of size and weight. The development of emergent units or projects of this nature is more fully discussed in the context of science education in chapter 8. Regardless of how many children or how much time is committed to the inquiry process, the idea that children take an active role in generating and answering their own questions is an effective strategy for differentiating the curriculum in ways that will give exceptionally bright children a meaningful challenge.

Increase Complexity

One of the most obvious yet most difficult ways of differentiating the curriculum to challenge exceptionally bright children is to increase the complexity of the concepts we are teaching. We may know we need to make the content of our curriculum "harder," but how do we do it? Beth and Claire, for example, in teaching their unit on pets, prepared to teach concepts and information about animals at a level appropriate for most preschool children. How do they make these concepts more complex for children like Maria and Nathan?

A helpful tool for measuring the complexity of the concepts and experiences we are providing for children is Bloom's taxonomy (Bloom 1974). The taxonomy is a tool created by the educational psychologist Benjamin Bloom to help teachers define learning objectives that promote higher-order thinking. By "higher order" we mean thinking with increasing complexity and creativity. Bloom's taxonomy, as revised and updated by Lorin Anderson and David Krathwohl (2001), has six levels, with the first level representing the least complex thought and each level thereafter involving greater thought abstraction and sophistication:

1. **Remembering.** When children remember, they are recalling and restating information.

2. **Understanding.** When children understand, they are able to explain an idea using their own words.

3. **Applying.** When children apply, they are using the information in a new way.

4. **Analyzing.** When children analyze, they are questioning or testing the information or ideas they've gained.

5. **Evaluating.** When children evaluate, they are determining the value of information or ideas.

6. **Creating.** When children create, they are using what they've learned to develop something completely new.

Bloom's taxonomy can be used to make sure a curriculum plan is challenging children at every level, to benefit not just the exceptionally bright children but all the children. To illustrate, consider how Beth and Claire could use Bloom's taxonomy to evaluate their pet unit as to whether they are challenging children to use higher-order thinking skills.

1. **Remembering.** During the "morning meeting," Claire and Beth ask questions (*What kinds of animals make good pets? What does a veterinarian do?*). When children answer these questions, they are restating information they learned through their own experience, books, and discussion.

2. **Understanding.** When Claire and Beth invite children to dictate a story at the literacy table, the stories the children tell about pets demonstrate their understanding of what pets need and how people take care of their pets. When a child dictates, "I have a cat named Cheezits. We give her food in a dish on the floor," she is demonstrating her understanding of pets and their needs.

3. **Applying.** During free play, a few children are building a structure out of blocks. Beth observes their play for a few minutes and then asks, "What are you building?" One of the children replies, "A store." Beth asks, "What kind of store are you building?" The child answers, "We don't know yet." Beth recognizes this as an opportunity for children to apply what they have been learning about pets to their block play. She gently suggests, "I wonder if you could make it a pet store." The children seem to like Beth's idea. They use the blocks to designate different spaces for different kinds of pet products, such as leashes for dogs and cages for birds. Their play demonstrates what they have learned about pets through stories and discussion and how they are applying it to something new, constructing a pet store.

4. **Analyzing.** One way children analyze new information is by comparing one thing to another. At the games table, when children sort dog and cat counters, they are comparing cats to dogs. Claire asks the children questions that encourage this analysis. "How are dogs and cats the same?" she asks. One child responds, "Dogs and cats both have tails, but cat tails don't wag." An exceptionally bright child may need the challenge of comparing a greater number of variables, for instance, textures of fur or ability to swim.

5. **Evaluating.** In the dramatic play area, where the children have created an animal hospital, some children want to pretend to be cats and others want to pretend to be dogs. In deciding which role to take on, they are evaluating the roles. When Beth visits the dramatic play area, she asks them questions that challenge them to evaluate the choices they made. "Why did you decide to be a cat?" Maria responds, "Cats don't have to go outside in the winter. They can pee-pee in a box. I want to stay cozy, so I'm a cat." Her answer reflects an evaluation of the benefits of the role of a cat.

6. **Creating.** As the pet unit progresses, Beth and Claire continue to invite children to dictate stories at the literacy table, encouraging them to create stories about imaginary pets. Many of the stories the children dictate are completely original. Stories of fiction or make-believe demonstrate ways that many of the children are taking in a variety of information and ideas about pets and creating something new. (*Once upon a time there was a dog world where only dogs could be. Everybody barked at each other. Bark! Bark! Bark! No one could ever talk, but they all knew what to do.*)

After using Bloom's taxonomy to look at their pet unit, Beth and Claire can be more intentional about creating learning experiences at every level, from the most simple to the most complex. The good news is that intentionally creating opportunities for higher-level thinking will benefit not just the brightest children. It will benefit everyone in the class.

Strategies for Differentiating Teaching Practices

How we teach—our instructional practices—can also be differentiated to meet the individual needs of the children in our classrooms. Two of the best teaching practices that will help you differentiate to challenge exceptionally bright children have to do with how you group children and how you pace the curriculum and activities.

Create Flexible Groups

One important differentiation strategy is creating flexible groups. This means that teachers create groups based on children's interests *and* their abilities. The groups are called "flexible" because they are temporary. There is an understanding that abilities and interests shift and change rapidly and that children should not be "tracked" by having to stay in the same group assignment over a long period of time.

So, for example, in the pet unit, Beth and Claire may want to create a flexible group of advanced learners in order to present the children in that group with more challenging activities, materials, or conversations. Beth and Claire may decide to divide the whole class into flexible groupings, or they could create a hybrid configuration incorporating both choice activities and flexible grouping. A flexible group could be made up of Maria, Nathan, and Rashaad, another child who has demonstrated in his play that he already knows a lot about animals but doesn't yet have the vocabulary and language development to express what he knows. Grouping Rashaad with Nathan and Maria, who have more advanced vocabularies, will benefit Rashaad because he will be exposed to Nathan's and Maria's advanced language skills. The grouping will also benefit Nathan and Maria because Rashaad has knowledge, ideas, and questions about animals that will be new to them. Beth could meet with these three children at the literacy table and work on a special project with them, such as creating a book that lists and describes different breeds of dogs. Rashaad could draw the pictures, Maria could write the words (with support from Beth), and Nathan, who has prior knowledge of dog breeds, could dictate and explain the names of the breeds and their characteristics.

Adapt the Pace

Another way to differentiate teaching practices is to play with time. You can adapt the pace of a specific activity or adapt the pace of a whole curriculum unit. A faster pace to an activity such as a game challenges students by demanding greater expertise and faster thinking. A faster pace to a curriculum unit means more information and concepts are covered over a shorter period of time, preventing boredom and maximizing learning.

In the case of the pet unit, the children with a more advanced knowledge of pets, such as Maria and Nathan, would be allowed and encouraged to move on from the pet activities involving dogs and cats and begin to learn about more exotic pets, for instance, birds and reptiles. If Maria or Nathan appear to fidget and seem bored during a class discussion about dogs and cats, they could be allowed to sit off to the side and look at picture books related to other pets.

Sometimes slowing the pace can add challenge too, if slowing down means adding more depth and detail to an activity or curriculum sequence. Suppose Maria visits the literacy table and begins working on the words and illustrations for a pet book. Maria's teacher, Claire, notices that Maria has written the letter C at the top of one page and is drawing a picture of a cat. Claire comments, "Maria, this page reminds me of an alphabet book, with one page for each letter of the alphabet. Would you be interested in making your own alphabet book?"

Maria exclaims, "That's a great idea! I want to make an alphabet book about pets!"

Claire helps Maria make a plan for her book by setting aside twenty-six pieces of paper and showing Claire how to label each page and staple the papers together. When it's time to clean up and have snack, Maria begins to cry, "But I'm just getting started!" she exclaims. "I'll never have time to finish my alphabet book."

Claire differentiates for Maria by using several strategies to create opportunities for Maria to finish her book. First, she lets Maria continue working on her book a few extra minutes by asking her coteacher, Beth, to call Maria last for washing hands for snack. Claire also gives Maria a special folder for storing or "saving" the pages of her alphabet book. During snacktime, Claire has a conversation with Maria about how much time she will need to finish the book, creating an impromptu math lesson.

"Maria," Claire asks. "How many pages of your alphabet book did you finish today?"

"I did three," responds Maria. "I did A and B and C."

"So if you do three pages a day, I wonder how many days it will take you to finish your book."

Maria does not yet have the math skills to figure out the answer, but she seems intrigued by the question. "Lots of days," she says.

"Okay," says Claire. "You can do a little bit at a time until you finish it." Over the next two weeks, Maria not only continues working on her alphabet book but also monitors her progress by using a tally sheet to count the number of pages she's completed each day. Claire has differentiated her teaching practices to create multiple learning opportunities that challenge Maria as well as the other children in the class, who have the opportunity to observe Maria.

Strategies for Differentiating the Learning Environment

How we set up our learning environments, including how we present and organize the materials in the classrooms, can also play a key role in differentiation to meet the needs of all the children and to challenge especially bright children. The primary methods for using the environment for differentiation are offering choices and adapting the materials.

Offer Choices

Offering choices is one of the best strategies for differentiation because when children make their own choices we can be confident that the learning experiences are aligned with their interests. This alignment means learning will be more meaningful to the children. Choices also allow children to take a more active role in their own learning because the decision-making process engages them and increases their sense of responsibility for what happens in the classroom.

One of the best ways to offer choices to children is to create learning experiences at "centers" and invite children to choose which center they want to visit. For the pet unit, Claire and Beth might use the existing areas of their pre-K classroom—the literacy corner, the block area, the dramatic play area, and the games table—and create pet-related activities in each area that in some way utilize the materials and activities already available there. Or they might create temporary centers, perhaps at tables or on the floor, that are specific to just this pet unit.

Choice, as a differentiation strategy, occurs when children are invited to make a decision about which center they want to visit. Authentic choice occurs when children are not steered in a certain direction. Also, choice works best when there are very broad time limits for each activity. If, for example, children are made to change or rotate through centers every twenty minutes, they are not really being given an authentic choice. Ideally, if a child makes a choice to pursue a specific learning experience, that decision is respected by allowing the child to stay in that area as long as her attention is held (within reasonable limits). With this in mind, Claire and Beth plan for four different centers that will introduce children to the unit.

All the children will be invited to choose a center during morning free play. For Maria and Nathan, the children who have already met the learning outcomes for this pet unit, being offered this choice is especially important for several reasons. The decision-making process will demonstrate to their teachers what direction to take their learning. Maria, for example, chooses the literacy table. Even though she already has advanced literacy skills, her choice shows

Plan Title: Pet Unit Learning Centers

Literacy: Pet books and pet stories
Materials:
- a table where a variety of pet picture books, both fiction and nonfiction, is available to look at or read
- lined paper and fat pencils in a basket

Notes:
One of the teachers will oversee this table, reading to children and taking story dictation.

Blocks: Build a pet store
Materials:
- a floor rug surrounded by shelves full of wooden unit blocks
- a bin of toy animals the teachers have added: dogs, cats, fish, birds, and mice

Notes:
The teachers offer an open-ended invitation that the block area is a place to "build a pet store."

Dramatic Play: Animal hospital
Materials:
- a small table and chairs and some wooden play kitchen furniture
- toy animals, toy doctor kits, and several lab coats, a telephone, and an old laptop computer

Notes:
The teachers offer an open-ended invitation that the dramatic play area is an animal hospital where the children can take care of sick and hurt animals.

Games Table: Counting and sorting pets
Materials:
- a small table with several sets of "counters," small plastic toys in three colors (blue, red, and yellow) shaped like dogs and cats
- a stack of oversize graph paper (one-inch squares) and markers in a basket
- a laminated numeral chart showing the numerals 1 through 10

Notes:
The other teacher will oversee this table. She will invite children to sort or "make piles" of the counters and observe the choices they make. Some children will sort by category (dogs or cats), while others will sort by color. She will invite children to count the pets in each group and show them how to record what they have found out on paper using numerals, tallies, or drawings.

that she wants to continue to deepen and expand her ability to understand and tell stories. Nathan, who chooses the games table rather than the animal hospital, demonstrates through his choice that he is interested in new, unfamiliar concepts. He is not interested in deepening his already extensive knowledge of what happens in animal hospitals, at least not today. His focus seems to be on exploring new math concepts as they relate to a familiar topic, pets.

Adapt the Materials

Another way to differentiate the classroom environment for more advanced learners is to adapt the classroom materials in a way that creates a more challenging experience for the exceptionally bright children. There are three primary ways we can adapt the materials: we can add something, we can take something away, or we can replace materials. Any of these three options can increase the level of challenge.

Add Something

Most early childhood teachers already have some kind of experience with differentiating by adding materials to accommodate the individual needs of the child, though they may not realize it was differentiation. For example, have you ever let a child hold a toy during story time to help him sit still and listen? Other children may have noticed and asked, "Why does James get to hold a toy? I want to hold a toy, too." A wise teacher knows it's okay to respond, "James gets to hold a toy because this is a special plan for James. It's what he needs right now."

Adding something can be a helpful differentiation strategy to meet the needs of an exceptionally bright child. Say that Maria, who already knows how to count to ten, chooses to visit the games table. The materials available at that table include:

- a small table with several sets of "counters," small plastic toys in three colors (blue, red, and yellow) shaped like dogs and cats
- a stack of oversize graph paper (one-inch squares) and markers in a basket
- a laminated numeral chart showing the numerals 1 through 10

What could you add to this table to extend Maria's learning and challenge her to count beyond ten? One option would be to increase the quantity of counters, taking care to make sure there were at least twenty-five of each animal. Another option might be to add a piece of equipment that would challenge Maria to count to ten in other ways, for instance, with an abacus, a ruler, or a calculator. A teacher could present these materials to Maria in a mini-lesson with one-on-one instructions for how to use the equipment. Or they could be offered in an open-ended, exploratory way. "Here's something that helps people count. Can you think of ways people might use it?"

Take Something Away

Sometimes the best way to make a task more difficult is to take something away. The children are challenged to accomplish the task with less material or information and they need to think creatively, making connections and drawing conclusions in order to finish a task. One example of this is asking a child to complete a wooden puzzle without using the frame.

In the case of Maria at the games table, the removal of the laminated chart would challenge her to remember and order the numerals on her own, without a model. By the same token, if Maria visits the literacy table, taking away the pet books, which serve as examples and inspiration for the children, might help challenge Maria to come up with her own ideas, and to recall and apply her knowledge of letters and words without having the model of the books for reference.

Replace the Materials

Another way to adapt the materials in order to differentiate for advanced learners is to replace the materials with something entirely new. In the case of the games table, the animal counters could be replaced with a board game, such as Parcheesi, that requires both counting and strategy. At the literacy table, a computer and keyboard could replace writing materials, and Maria could be invited to type her stories instead of writing them. Replacing materials with other items would probably not be a routine decision, only an occasional accommodation for a child who has truly exhausted all the possibilities of learning from the materials that are already available. If an exceptionally bright child is offered alternative materials and other children express an interest in using those materials too, this would be a great opportunity for the exceptionally bright child to demonstrate what he knows and socialize with another child by helping to introduce that child to the new materials.

Conversation: Asking Questions and Providing Authentic Feedback

Chapter 4

Classroom Conversations

As early childhood professionals, we know classroom conversations are important. Every day we use a variety of communication strategies to manage the classroom and support children's social-emotional development. We acknowledge children's feelings (*I know you're sad when Mommy says good-bye*), we support their decisions (*Helping Jaden with the blocks was a great choice*), and we guide them in conflict resolution (*Let's think of a way we can make enough room on the rug for everyone to sit down*). We know the importance of intentional communication in creating a positive and constructive classroom environment.

Our communication strategies can also play a critical role in specifically supporting children's cognitive engagement and development. Think how often in your own experience you've discovered a new idea or perspective simply through talking with other people. The questions they asked or the direction they took the conversation may have led you to a new or deeper understanding of a problem, situation, or concept. Conversation can work this way for young children as well.

The conversations that take place between teacher and child can help develop higher-order—or more complex—thinking skills. Two examples of this include creative thinking, which is thinking with flexibility and considering

A conversation between teacher and child would shed light on the child's thinking behind this drawing and reveal that the child created a pattern of swing sets.

possibilities beyond just one right answer, and critical thinking, which involves questioning common assumptions and reflecting on and evaluating information. Developing these higher-order thinking skills can contribute significantly to greater enjoyment of learning as well as academic success in the elementary years and beyond.

Through conversations, young children can begin to or further develop these higher-order thinking skills and begin to recognize themselves as learners and problem solvers. Teachers and caregivers can be intentional about guiding conversations toward this goal. This kind of intentional teaching benefits all children, but it can be especially important for challenging exceptionally bright young children, who undoubtedly already have begun developing higher-order thinking skills and are usually more than ready to participate in complex conversations that exercise their skills.

Metacognition

When we become aware of our own thinking—such as the child who exclaims, "Hey, I just got a great idea!"—we are experiencing what's called "metacognition." The process of metacognition is an example of higher-order thinking. Most young children are just beginning to develop this ability. To think about our thinking, to become aware of our own learning process, requires language, reflection, and abstract thought.

To understand the value of conversations, it's important to understand the role of metacognition. Metacognition is an important learning tool for both children and adults because it allows us to control and plan our own learning. When we think and talk about what's going on in our brains, we are noticing and evaluating our own thinking strategies as well as making conscious choices about where we direct our attention. Metacognition allows us to intentionally make connections between new information and what we already know.

Using Bloom's Taxonomy to Promote Higher-Order Thinking

Bloom's taxonomy, as described in chapter 3, provides a helpful structure for understanding and measuring the levels of complexity and depth in a learning experience. In summary, Bloom (1974) asserted that remembering and understanding involve the least complex thought processes. Applying and analyzing are more complex. And the most complex, or highest, level of thinking is that involved with evaluating and creating.

Bloom's taxonomy

To further illustrate these levels of complexity, think about how a child's understanding of a single concept grows over time. The following case study is about a child learning to understand the idea that there is no school on the weekend and the implications of that schedule for her life. She starts by remembering that some days aren't school days.

1. Remembering

At breakfast, three-year-old Ginny asks her mother, "Am I going to school today?"

Her mother responds, "No, it's the weekend. Today is Saturday. There's no school today."

Later, after breakfast is over, Ginny asks again, "Is there school today?"

Her mother replies, "We talked about that at breakfast this morning. Do you remember?"

Ginny replies, "Yes, there's no school today."

This is Bloom's first level of thinking, "Remembering." Ginny recalls the correct information but still needs to repeat her question, "Am I going to school today?" throughout the day.

2. Understanding

As Ginny grows a bit older, she begins to recognize the weekly pattern of weekdays at school and weekend days at home. One Saturday morning at breakfast Ginny asks, "Mama, is today the weekend?"

"Yes, Ginny," her mother replies. "It's Saturday."

"Then there's no school today, right?" Ginny asks.

"Yes," says her mother. "That's right."

"Understanding" is Bloom's second level of thinking. Ginny now realizes without being reminded that there's no school on the weekend.

3. Applying

As a four-year-old, Ginny begins applying what she knows about weekends to other ideas and experiences. One Saturday morning, Ginny says to her mother, "I'm going to wear my pretty sandals today."

"Yes, your sandals are very nice, aren't they?"

"My sandals are my prettiest shoes of all. But I'm not allowed to wear sandals to school, am I, Mama?"

"That's right, sweetie. You have to wear tie shoes to school."

Ginny nods. "But I can wear my sandals today because it's the weekend."

This is Bloom's third level of thinking, "Applying." Ginny has taken her knowledge of shoes and applied it to her understanding about what happens on the weekends.

4. Analyzing

As Ginny grows and learns, she begins to compare weekdays with weekends. This is an example of her ability to use an even higher order of thinking, analyzing.

One day Ginny says to her mother, "Keisha is my very best friend and Becca is my medium best friend."

"Why is that?" asks Ginny's mother.

"Because Keisha is my friend at school and Becca is my friend on the weekends. And I have more school days than I have weekend days. So I have more days with Keisha so she's my very best friend."

Ginny uses "Analyzing," the fourth level of Bloom's taxonomy, to determine that she spends more time with Keisha, her school friend, than with Becca, her weekend friend.

5. Evaluating

The next cognitive milestone is Ginny's ability to evaluate her understanding of the idea that there is no school on the weekend. This level involves critical thinking, the ability to question previous beliefs or assumptions. This leap in Ginny's understanding occurs one Saturday when she discovers that she left her favorite doll, Marigold, in her cubby at school.

"Mama, Mama! We have to go to school today!"

"But, Ginny, it's Saturday. There's no school today."

"But I left Marigold in my cubby and I need her."

"I'm sorry, sweetie. The school is closed today."

"That's a stupid, stupid rule, Mama! Why does the school have to close, anyway? Why can't it just stay open every day? Let's go anyway, Mama. Take me to school today."

"No one's there today, sweetie. The teachers are at home."

"Then let's go to Miss Johnson's house and get the key from her and then go to the school and get Marigold."

"I don't think we can do that, sweetie."

"But, Mama, we'd take the key right back again!"

"Evaluating" is Bloom's fifth level of thinking. Ginny now understands that there is no school on Saturday, but she is not happy about it. She uses critical thinking to articulate both a reason for going to school and a method for gaining access to the school.

6. Creating

The ability to create something new, to synthesize an idea and turn it into something all your own, demonstrates the highest level of cognitive development. Ginny's experience leaving Marigold at school motivates her to evaluate her understanding of what happens on the weekends and to use her new depth of knowledge to create something completely new.

"Mama, look what I made."

"Oh, it's a beautiful drawing. What is it?"

"It's a calendar. It shows all the days my school is open and all the days my school is closed."

"I see. It looks like you made a square for each day. Just like the school calendar on our refrigerator."

"Right. But my calendar is better."

"How is your calendar better?"

"Mine shows who gets the key."

"What key?"

"The key to the school, Mama. In my calendar, kids get to borrow the key to the school and take turns locking it up. Then if anybody ever forgets anything, somebody can always open the door."

Ginny's calendar demonstrates "Creating," the highest level of thinking, according to Bloom. She has taken everything she's learned, synthesized it, and created something unique that represents her own ideas and opinions.

Tools for Building Conversations

As described in chapter 3, we can use Bloom's taxonomy as a tool for developing and evaluating the curriculum, ensuring that the content is challenging to exceptionally bright young children. We can also use Bloom's taxonomy as a tool for developing conversations and questions that invite higher-order thinking such as metacognition. This kind of intentional teaching benefits all children, but it can be especially important for challenging exceptionally bright young children, who thrive when they participate in conversations that involve complex thinking. Three of the most important conversational tools that can be used intentionally toward that end are:

- asking questions
- listening
- providing feedback

at might take place between a teacher   chool classroom. It demonstrates the   tools.

le a bed for my bunny.

f three blocks. Your bunny looks very   it how you made that bed. How did   e the right size for your bunny? (ask-

le.

first. (listening) How did you know   king questions)

the top.

Teacher: I see. (listening) You saw that her ears were longer than the bed. (providing feedback) Was that when you figured out you would need to add a block and make the bed three blocks longs? (asking questions)

Child: Yup.

Teacher: And now the bed is just right for the bunny. (providing feedback) Or could you make it even better? (asking questions)

Child: Hmm. I could make it softer.

Teacher: Softer? (listening) Yes, bunny might like that. (providing feedback) How would you make it softer? (asking questions)

Child: I'll use the towel to make a pillow.

When used together, as it is natural to do, the three strategies form a powerful and fruitful combination in support of children's complex thinking. But each strategy is important in its own right. Each can be used intentionally in the classroom to support children's cognitive development.

Asking Questions

Asking questions is an effective practice to encourage young children to think in more complex ways. Some of the questions we ask are "closed" and some are "open," or "open-ended." Closed questions have a single correct answer, whereas open-ended questions tend to encourage more detailed and complex answers from children.

TABLE 5.1: Closed and Open Questions

Examples of closed questions:	Examples of open-ended questions:
How many blocks did you use?	What do you think would happen if you took that block away?
Does a round block have corners?	If you wanted to add a roof, how would you build it?
How many wings do birds usually have?	Why do birds build nests?
What time does school start?	What can people do to keep from being late?
Does rain only happen at night?	How did you know it might rain today?

The value of using open-ended questions in an early childhood classroom is well known. This does not mean, however, that a closed question, a question that has a specific right or wrong answer, is not useful. If a child is creating a pattern with Unifix cubes, for instance, the teacher may ask, "What color comes next in the pattern?" There's only one right answer, so this is a closed question. It can be a helpful question, though, because it draws a distracted child's attention to the important characteristics that form the pattern, or because the question assesses the child's current understanding of patterns.

A closed question can be paired with an open-ended question to challenge the child further and promote higher-order thinking. For example, "What color comes next in the pattern?" is an excellent introduction to one of the most powerful open-ended questions you can ask children: "How do you know?"

The question "How do you know?" draws children's attention to their own thinking and their own learning process; it also promotes metacognition. The process of answering the question is an opportunity for children to describe how they know what they know. By bringing the thought process, the problem-solving process, out into the light of day, by explaining it with words, you encourage children to begin to develop the tools and the thinking strategies that they can draw on again and again.

Suppose the child says, "I know red is next because the pattern is blue and red." The conversation does not have to end here. The teacher can continue the process with another pair of closed and open questions. Or perhaps begin with a statement. "I hear you say that the pattern is blue and red. I see blue and red, too. How many blues and how many reds form the pattern?" The child may then notice that the pattern consists of one red followed by two blues. The closed question draws the child's attention to the fact that the pattern consists not only of colors but also of varying numbers of cubes in each color.

The child's answer to the closed question, "Two blues. But just one red," then allows the teacher to follow up with an open-ended question, "What do you think will happen if you continue this pattern?" This question is deliberately ambiguous. The child could take it in several directions. The child may simply say, "There will be one red, two blues, one red, two blues, one red, two blues." Or (and here's an exciting possibility) the child may answer the question with a statement or idea that demonstrates the possibility of more complex thinking. "If I keep making this pattern, we'll run out of blue cubes." And, again, the open-ended question can follow: "How do you know?"

The interesting difference between "There will be one red, two blues . . ." and "we'll run out of blue cubes" is that the second statement demonstrates higher-order thinking—thinking that requires deeper, more complex thought processes. The child has drawn a conclusion and made a prediction. She is not just reporting the facts; she is interpreting them in a meaningful way. The teacher's open-ended question helped spark the child's thinking.

Questions That Increase Complexity

In the classroom, we can use Bloom's taxonomy as a guide for asking questions that prompt children to use higher-order thinking skills. Suppose a pair of four-year-olds, Dylan and Olivia, are in the block area building with large, hollow wooden blocks. Using Bloom's taxonomy as a guide, here are questions you might ask that would raise the level of complexity and challenge the children to use higher-order thinking skills.

1. Remembering

Teacher: What are you building?
Olivia: A boat.
Teacher: What kind of boat?
Dylan: A big ship.

2. Understanding

Teacher: What are the parts of your ship?
Dylan: Here's where we sit.
Olivia: I'm making the sail.

3. Applying

Teacher: What will you do with your ship when it's finished?
Olivia: Sail it on the water.
Dylan: To the ocean. To the beach.
Olivia: Right. We're sailing it across the ocean.

4. Analyzing

Teacher: So why did you choose to sail across the ocean in a ship instead of flying across the ocean in an airplane? (Both children shrug.)

Dylan: I don't know.

Teacher: Well, how is a boat better than an airplane?

Olivia: Because of the sail.

Teacher: You like having a sail?

Olivia: We can steer it with a sail.

Dylan: And! And you can get wet in the waves.

5. Evaluating

Teacher: How will you know when your ship is ready to sail?

Olivia: When the sail is done.

Teacher: How will you know when the sail is done?

Dylan: When it's here. (pointing up)

Teacher: When it's tall enough?

Dylan: Yeah. When it's up high.

Teacher: How high does the sail need to be?

Olivia: Tall enough to steer.

Teacher: As tall as a person?

Olivia: Taller. Even more taller than a person.

6. Creating

Teacher: How will you make your sail?

Dylan: We're making it now. It's bigger and bigger.

Teacher: What else do you need to build it?

Olivia: We need a cloth for the wind.

Teacher: What can you use for a cloth?

Olivia: I don't know, but we need it.

Dylan: We need a nap blanket. That can be the sail.

Olivia: Right! We need it.

Conversations That Describe Thinking

When we challenge children to describe their own thinking, we are helping them develop metacognition. Teachers and caregivers can do this by asking questions using specific cue words and phrases that point attention to the thinking process. We can call these types of cues and phrases "the language of learning." Examples include:

- "What do you think?"
- "How do you know?"
- "Why did you say that?"
- "What choice did you make?"
- "How did you figure that out?"

When teachers and caregivers ask these kinds of questions, children are challenged to reflect on and describe their own thinking. Teachers may also assist children in this process by giving them words to describe their thinking or using a combination of prompts and questions to draw out the child's words and ideas. Suppose three-year-old Sophia is served pear slices at snacktime:

Sophia: Apples! Yum!

Teacher: They look a little like apples, Sophia, but these are pear slices.

Sophia: I don't like pears.

Teacher: Have you ever tried pears, Sophia?

Sophia: No.

Teacher: Well, let's think about apples and pears. When I handed you the pear slices, you said, "Apples!" Do the pear slices look like apples?

Sophia: Yes.

Teacher: Are they the same color?

Sophia: (pointing) This part is the same but this part is different.

Teacher: The main part of the fruit is the same color, mostly white. But the skin is different. What color is the skin of the pear?

Sophia: Yellow.

Teacher: What color is the skin of an apple?

Sophia: Red.

Teacher: Yes, often an apple is red. And what's this brown thing there? (pointing)

Sophia: A seed?

Teacher: Yes, pears have seeds. Do apples have seeds? (Sophia nods.) So apples and pears both have seeds. Let's smell the pear and find out what it smells like. (Sophia sniffs the pear slice, then pops it in her mouth.)

Teacher: (laughing) Hey, where's the pear?

Sophia: I ate it!

Teacher: Why did you change your mind about eating it?

Sophia: Because it smelled wet, like an apple.

The questions the teacher asks draw Sophia's attention to the fact that she, Sophia, is making decisions and to the process she uses to evaluate the choices that she makes. Sophia demonstrates metacognition in several different ways. She is making connections between what she already knows (apples) and new information (pears). She makes two decisions: first, to not eat the pear and, later, to try it. Without the teacher's questions and commentary, Sophia would probably not have been aware of her own thinking. The conversation challenged Sophia to think and talk about what was going on in her head.

As educators, we can also model metacognition in the ways we talk about our own thinking. When a teacher says, "I'm wondering how we know if we have enough time to read all three stories today," she is using the language of learning and drawing attention to the process she uses to make decisions and solve problems. Shari Tishman and David Perkins (1997) of Harvard's Project Zero encourage teachers to use "thinking words" during their interactions with children, words such as:

- believe
- know
- guess
- reason
- imagine
- predict
- wonder
- prove

Using the language of learning to promote metacognition will challenge the exceptionally bright children in your classroom, but all the children benefit as well. This emphasis on the thinking process promotes creativity and exploration for all young children because it shifts the focus from being "right" or "wrong" to being a community of thinkers who have ideas.

Helpful Hints

In the rush of a busy day, it can sometimes be hard to think of good questions to ask. It may be helpful to memorize a few good sentence starters that can help get a conversation going: "I'm wondering . . . " and "Tell me about . . ." It is also helpful to have a few good follow-up questions on the tip of your tongue, such as, "How do you know?" and "Why do you think . . . ?"

Also, don't be afraid to leave some questions unanswered. There will always be questions you ask and questions children ask you that they and you don't yet have answers for. These might be sparks for an emerging curriculum topic or simply questions that the children are still thinking about. You can create a poster or bulletin board to serve as a "parking lot" for questions that are still in process. This also serves to demonstrate to the children that you, the adult, do not always know all the answers and that you value the process of asking questions and seeking answers.

Listening

Sometimes the most difficult part of asking questions is listening to the answers. There are few environments that are more distracting than a room full of young children. It's hard to stop, slow down, and tune in to one child. But, as mentioned in chapter 2, listening well to children is a profoundly important way to get to know and engage with them. Sometimes all it takes to really listen is making the choice to do so. Be intentional. Decide to open your ears and focus on what the child is saying. At times when the distractions are great, you may need to practice some listening techniques. Here are six specific techniques for tuning in and listening to children.

1. **Breathe.** After you ask a question, pause and take a deep breath, then relax and breathe out. Let your shoulders fall as you exhale. Taking a moment to breathe like this will help you resist the impulse to jump in and interrupt a child while he is speaking. If a child needs a moment to think before answering your question, breathing also helps you pause and wait, allowing the child the time he needs to ponder and collect his thoughts and ideas.

2. **Count to ten.** One way to be intentional about listening and giving children a chance to think and speak is to count silently to ten before you speak. This technique is especially helpful when asking questions of children who are reluctant to speak or who have difficulty with language, for instance, children with delays in language development or

children who are dual-language learners. These ten-second pauses are gifts to quiet children. The space gives them time to form their thoughts, search for words, and get ready to speak.

3. **Create a listening plan.** If you work with other adults, such as coteachers or assistant teachers, make a plan for how and when you will give children special attention, asking questions and tuning in to their answers. If you are going to be introducing some interesting new items at the science table, say, a bird's nest, make a plan with your coteacher to take turns supervising the classroom so one of you can sit at the table and ask children questions about what they see, think, and wonder about the bird's nest.

4. **Get comfortable.** It's hard to listen when you're walking, bending, cold, or hungry. When you are ready to tune in and really listen to children, get comfortable. Sit down and relax. When you are at ease and comfortable, children will follow your lead. And when children are comfortable they will be more likely to express their thoughts and ideas.

5. **Look at the child.** One of the best ways to show that you are really listening and giving someone your full attention is by looking at the other person's face. Position yourself at the child's level. Observe the child's body language, how he moves his hands as he speaks, his gestures, and his posture. Sometimes children tell us more with their bodies than with their words.

6. **Repeat back what the child has said.** Another useful listening technique is repeating the words the child has said. Repeating can be word for word, almost as if you are making a recording of the child and playing it back for her.

> Teacher: What do you see when you look at the bird's nest?
> Child: Sticks. Sticks in the muddy glue.
> Teacher: Yes, sticks in the muddy glue.

Repeating a child's words can also be a way to extend a child's ideas, building toward new understanding.

> Teacher: What do you see when you look at the bird's nest?
> Child: Sticks. Sticks in the muddy glue.
> Teacher: Yes, the mud seems to hold the sticks together like glue. That's an interesting idea.

Experiment with repeating a child's words. Sometimes repeating word for word works well, because it reassures children that you are truly listening and accepting their answers. Sometimes repeating and extending works well, when a child is ready to take the conversation to the next level.

Giving Authentic Feedback

In the field of gifted education, one of the common complaints of older children—students in elementary, middle, and high school—who are academically advanced is that their teachers rarely offer them feedback that is constructive and useful. Gifted students often hear praise (*Great job on that test!*) and compliments (*You're so good at math, you could teach this class!*), but they rarely hear specific feedback that will challenge them to try harder or direct them toward further exploration and learning. The same is true for young children who are exceptionally bright. Adults, both parents and teachers, often tell them how smart they are, but if they are already meeting age-appropriate expectations, such as writing their name or counting to ten, they are usually not given ideas or direction for what they can learn next. Most preschool and prekindergarten educators are so focused on preparing children for kindergarten that we rarely think about what else, beyond readiness, we can offer children.

Beyond Praise

There is some debate among educators about the value of praise (Kohn 2012). Some feel that authentic praise (*I love your beautiful painting. You are such a talented artist!*) benefits children by helping build their self-esteem. Others feel that giving praise conditions children to seek acceptance from others and diminishes their ability to feel internal satisfaction from their accomplishments. Some research, such as the work of Carol Dweck of Stanford University, suggests that children who are frequently praised for their intelligence rather than for their effort become excessively focused on achieving the right answers and less interested in the process of exploring and learning (Mueller and Dweck 1998). My experience working with exceptionally bright children is that noticing and commenting on hard work and effort (*You spent a long time working on that puzzle. You didn't stop until every piece was in the right place.*) is a great way to reinforce the value of effort and encourage children to do their best.

Making statements that describe young children's play, their actions, and their efforts is one way to provide feedback to children; it helps them think more creatively and critically. Suppose Maya is playing with a toy xylophone. It has eight metal bars, one for each note in a scale, and a small mallet for striking the bars and making music. Maya has taken some small metal jingle bells and set them on top of the xylophone, one on each metal bar. She is now using the mallet to play the xylophone. Each time she strikes the xylophone there are two sounds: the note of the xylophone and the vibrating ring of the jingle bell. You notice that Maya keeps pausing and moving the bells around on the xylophone. You begin to suspect that Maya is less interested in making music and more interested in how the bells are affected by the movement and sound of the instrument.

Maya is conducting an experiment related to the physics of sound and movement. Her use of the xylophone and the bells, along with the concentration shown on her face, reveal a very deep curiosity about how the world works. The concentration and patience she demonstrates in the way she conducts these experiments are beyond what most preschool children are usually able to sustain.

What feedback could you give Maya that will challenge her to follow her passions and learn even more about sound, movement, and vibrations? You could simply acknowledge or praise her effort and creativity (*I like the way you experimented with placing the bells on top of the xylophone*). But that doesn't help Maya advance her knowledge and take her experiment to the next level. Maya really needs some content knowledge—some information that will help her understand what she is doing so she can make choices about how to continue to extend her understanding.

A good place to start is to make some very specific statements about what you observed, such as a series of statements that begin with "I noticed . . ." or "I saw . . ." or "It seemed like . . ." (*Maya, I watched what you were doing with the xylophone. I noticed that you put the bells on top of the metal bars. I saw how you hit the bars with the mallet and then moved the bells around. It seemed like you were listening carefully to the sounds you were making.*)

Statements like these support learning because they acknowledge and affirm the child's actions and they also help the child reflect on her own behavior. It's like playing back a movie so the child can see herself through your eyes. Observing children and making statements that describe what they are doing is a valuable way to give children feedback. These statements and descriptions also set the stage for the asking of questions. Perhaps the statements about Maya's experiment could be followed by some good open-ended questions (*Why did you choose to put the bells on top of the xylophone? What happened when you hit the xylophone with the mallet? What did you hear? What did you see?*).

Taking It to the Next Level

To give children feedback that will help them take their learning to the next level, you will have to reflect and draw some conclusions about what they really want to learn. The observations and conversation with Maya seem to reveal that she is behaving more like a scientist than a musician. She isn't making up a song; she is exploring the physics of movement and sound. Maya needs some support to learn the vocabulary and concepts that will help progress her explorations. One possibility would be to introduce Maya to the word "vibrations" and draw her attention to the vibrations that the xylophone bars and the bells make. You could suggest that, as she continues her experiment, she try touching the xylophone or the bells immediately after she strikes the bars with the mallet and see if she can feel the vibrations. Once Maya becomes aware of the connections between vibrations and sounds, there are any number of other directions she could take her explorations.

Sometimes thinking of these next steps for exceptionally bright children takes a little research on the part of the teacher. In Maya's case, you might not have any previous knowledge of music or the physics of music to draw upon. A little research, such as checking out a book from the library or talking to an expert, may be necessary for collecting information and ideas to challenge exceptionally bright young children with advanced knowledge and passionate interests.

Helping Children Set Their Own Learning Goals

Another way to ensure that exceptionally bright children will receive the feedback they need to continue to grow and learn is to hold them accountable for their own learning. When children become passionately interested in a topic or in mastering a skill, ask them to articulate what they want to do. Ask, "What do you want to learn?" or "What do you want to find out?" Explain to children that learning goals can be achieved over a long time and can be something they think about and work on for many days, weeks, months, or even years. Perhaps Maya expresses to you, "I want to know where music comes from." Write down the child's goal, post it in a journal or on the wall of the classroom, and share it with the child's family.

Once a child has articulated a learning goal, that goal can be regularly revisited and evaluated. Progress can be documented with words or photographs. The tracking of learning goals with tangible documents and "artifacts" such as drawings or projects allows children to share what they have learned and accomplished with their families and with other children. Suppose part of Maya's explorations includes making a guitar out of a shoebox and rubber bands. During a class gathering, for instance, a morning meeting or story time, Maya could demonstrate her guitar for the rest of the class. The other children could be encouraged to ask Maya questions about her guitar. The sharing of her progress with the other children adds another layer of feedback, in this case in the form of peer-to-peer dialogue. These kinds of conversations emphasize that all the children are part of a community of lifelong learners.

Connection: Helping Children Learn from Each Other

Better Together

In the field of gifted education, a common differentiation strategy for challenging academically advanced students in the primary grades is separating them from the general classroom for part of the day—"pullout" instruction—or placing them in a separate classroom that's only for gifted students. For many good reasons, these methods are rarely used in an early childhood setting. The first reason is that developmentally appropriate practice in early childhood education calls for a curriculum that supports the whole child through a smoothly integrated program that addresses social and physical development, as well as cognitive development. Exceptionally bright children have advanced cognitive development, but they still need a broad experience that prepares them not just for school but also for living in the world and getting along with other people. This is not to say that young children with advanced cognitive abilities should not participate in short-term enrichment experiences such as a special accelerated summer reading program. But most young children will best benefit from a core classroom experience that is part of a general early childhood program serving a diverse population of learners. An integrated curriculum is especially important for children with asynchronous development—those who excel in one area but may be lagging behind in another.

Another reason why exceptionally bright children should probably not be separated from their same-age peers in early childhood programs is that from birth to age five, the cognitive, physical, and social development domains are interrelated. For all young children, learning is not only a cognitive experience but also a physical and social experience. A constructivist approach, commonly accepted as best practice in early childhood education, emphasizes the connection between the cognitive and the physical. Constructivists assert the idea, as defined by theorist Jean Piaget, that children construct their own knowledge through hands-on, sensory experiences. Like the toddler who picks up a stick and puts it in her mouth, or the preschooler who runs his hand along the bark of a tree, young children develop their intellect, their understanding of the world, by moving their bodies and exploring their environment with all their senses. Exceptionally bright young children need these physical, sensory experiences just as much as their typically developing peers.

The interconnection between cognitive learning and social learning is one of the strongest arguments against "pulling out" exceptionally bright children from general early childhood classrooms. Learning is, at its heart, a living, breathing social experience. Exploration, experimentation, debate, discovery, and even making mistakes are all learning processes that happen not in isolation but in the spaces between people. Every early childhood classroom is a community of learners rich with opportunities for all children to learn from each other. These connections benefit exceptionally bright children because they provide opportunities to deepen learning and create new challenges.

Overview of Social Learning

Learning is a social experience. Children gain knowledge, skills, and ideas through conversations and interactions with both adults and other children. Moreover, social interactions play a key role in cognitive development. These are the essential ideas behind social learning theory. The social learning theorist Lev Vygotsky (1978, 57) stated, "Every function in the child's cultural development appears twice: first, on the social level, and later, on the individual level; first, *between* people (*interpsychological*) and then *inside* the child (*intrapsychological*)."

Children learn from their parents and teachers, but they also learn a lot from each other. Children are motivated to participate in learning activities when they see their friends and other children having fun and being successful. For example, during a preschool story time, the teacher may invite individual children to stand up and point to letters they recognize on a page in a picture book. Zach stands up and points out three letters he knows: A, C, and Z. Another child, Ben, who has not yet demonstrated much interest in or knowledge of letters, sees his friend Zach gain attention from the teacher and win the admiration of other children. Ben pays keen attention to Zach and watches carefully as Zach points to each letter. When the teacher asks for a second volunteer, Ben raises his hand and is invited to stand up. Ben is able to remember and identify the letter A that his role model, Zach, has pointed out. Ben proudly exclaims, "Here's the letter A!"

More Knowledgeable Other

In the example above, Zach, as Ben's role model, functions as what Vygotsky called a more knowledgeable other (MKO). Exceptionally bright children often function in this role for their same-age peers. The opportunity to serve as a role model is usually a positive experience both for the MKO and for the child who is learning from the MKO. Serving as an MKO is not the same thing as being assigned to tutor the other children or serve as a mini assistant teacher. MKOs are peers of the other children; they are their friends and equals. Their important function is to serve as collaborators and role models.

In a welcoming, inclusive learning community, the diversity of all the children's strengths and talents is nurtured and supported, and collaborative learning occurs frequently. While an exceptionally bright child may serve as a learning role model for some children, on other occasions other children will serve as role models for that exceptionally bright child in other areas of development.

Suppose these same two boys, Ben and Zach, are playing together on the playground. Ben asks Zach, "Do you want to be firebenders with me?"

"What's a firebender?" Zach replies.

"Like a dragon who uses fire for fighting. Except it's a people."

"Okay," says Zach. Ben begins running around the playground, making fiery whooshing sounds with his mouth. Zach runs after him, working hard to keep up with Ben and copy his agile jumps and turns.

Zach, with his advanced language and literacy skills, was the MKO for Ben during story time. But in the context of pretend play, Ben, who has more advanced motor skills and social skills, becomes the MKO for Zach. And even though Zach's cognitive development is more advanced than Ben's, Zach's friendship with Ben still provides opportunities for Zach to grow cognitively. For example, Ben and Zach's pretend play as firebenders may spark Zach's curiosity about dragons and legends about fire-breathing creatures. This could inspire Zach to seek out new and more challenging storybooks at school and during his family's visits to the library. Zach's advanced vocabulary and reading level, along with his ability to understand and remember complex plotlines, will allow him to contribute exciting new ideas to his pretend play with Ben. The conversations between Zach and Ben, as they talk about topics such as which dragons are the most powerful, will challenge Zach to explain and articulate his interpretation of the stories and inspire him to explore his ideas further.

Zone of Proximal Development and Scaffolding

Another Vygotskian concept that is helpful in understanding the rich potential for learning in a social context is the concept of the zone of proximal development, or ZPD. Vygotsky asserted that the ZPD is the distance between what a child is able to do on her own and what she is able to do with help. It is the role of the teacher to provide learning experiences for the child that are within that ZPD, experiences that are neither too easy, so that they can be accomplished without effort, nor too difficult, so that even with assistance they are completely overwhelming.

Teachers create optimal learning experiences for children in the ZPD by scaffolding learning. Scaffolding means providing supports, through instruction or through interactions with adults or more knowledgeable others, that gradually build knowledge and skills. Scaffolding may involve modeling, demonstration, direct instruction, or any number of other teaching methods. For example, in chapter 4, with Maya, the child exploring the physics of sound with a xylophone, scaffolding ideas for the educator included introducing the word "vibrations," defining the term, and demonstrating how vibrations can be felt each time the instrument is struck.

In my own experience, working with exceptionally bright children has expanded my beliefs about what young children can do and understand. I worked for many years with a general population of children in preschools and child care centers, but when I began to focus my work on exceptionally bright children (as the coordinator of an enrichment program that serves young children with advanced cognitive development), I was often surprised by how much the children already knew and what they were capable of learning and understanding. The ZPD for exceptionally bright children extended much further than I had ever anticipated. I have met children as young as three and four with the capacity for complex, abstract thought that goes well beyond what is described in any child development textbook.

The following are examples that demonstrate how far a child's ZPD can extend when learning is supported, or scaffolded, by both teachers and peers. Suppose Ms. Abby has set a curriculum goal or outcome that every child in her class will write a story. None of the children in her pre-K class, not even the most advanced learners, have both the small-motor skills and the literacy skills to write an entire story independently. But Ms. Abby can scaffold the task in a variety of ways to provide the supports necessary for every child, at a variety of different ability levels, to successfully participate in the task. To understand what happens next, take a look at four children in the class:

- Julia is able to write all twenty-six letters of the alphabet and has recently started sounding out words phonetically.
- David can write a few letters. He has not yet started sounding out words.
- Wyatt can draw pictures. He hasn't yet started writing letters.
- Nadine doesn't like to draw or write. She actively resists any attempts to direct her to the writing table.

As an intentional teacher, Ms. Abby has observed each of these children and created anecdotal notes describing their interests and abilities. Although Ms. Abby doesn't use the words "zone of proximal development" in her notes, she has essentially described the ZPD for each child. She knows what each child is capable of accomplishing independently, and she has a sense of what each child will probably be able to accomplish with assistance and supports. She also enters the classroom with an open mind, ready to adjust and expand her expectations if the children demonstrate they are capable of even more than she originally expected.

Julia and Wyatt

For Julia, the child who is able to write all the letters of the alphabet and has recently started sounding out short, two- and three-letter words, Ms. Abby's scaffolding strategy is to model the sounding out of increasingly complex words while encouraging Julia to use invented spelling. For example, Julia wants to write a story about a puppy and with her teacher's coaching she is able to spell "puppy" with the letters P-A-P-E. Through these scaffolding activities Julia is able to write a very short (three-sentence) story titled "3 PGZ AND POCE PAPE" ("Three Pigs and a Pokey Puppy"). Ms. Abby invites Julia to collaborate with Wyatt, the child who can draw pictures but is not yet writing letters, to create a poster that can be used to introduce Julia's story to the class. At first Julia is reluctant to work with Wyatt, preferring to work alone, but Ms. Abby points out to Julia that Wyatt has a puppy at home and he will bring that knowledge, along with his drawing expertise, to the project. Julia agrees and she works with Wyatt to plan and create the poster, which features Wyatt's drawing of a puppy with Julia's careful lettering announcing the title of the story. During group time, Wyatt holds the poster while Julia reads the story aloud to the group. The experience has stretched Julia's ability to work collaboratively with other children and deepened her understanding of the uses of print and the ways images and text can work together. The experience has also increased Wyatt's curiosity about writing, and with Julia as his role model he is now inspired to try writing titles and labels for his other drawings.

David and Nadine

For David, the child who can write a few letters but has not yet started sounding out words, Ms. Abby's primary scaffolding strategy is story dictation. (The practice of writing down stories children dictate is described at length in chapter 6.) Ms. Abby invites David to make up his own story and tell it to her so she can write it down. David begins telling a story about a magic hat, but he is soon distracted by his friend Nadine, who wants David to play with her. (Nadine is the child who doesn't like writing or drawing.) Ms. Abby lets David play with Nadine, but she takes a clipboard with paper and pencil and follows the children into the dramatic play area. When she observes David holding one of the hats in the dress-up bin, Ms. Abby asks, "Is that a magic hat, like in your story?" David smiles and puts the hat on his head. "Look, Nadine, it's a magic hat." Nadine replies, "Turn me into something! Make me a mouse!" As David and Nadine play, Ms. Abby writes down what she sees in the form of a brief story: "David put on a magic hat. He turned Nadine into a mouse. The mouse looked for cheese. The mouse said, 'I love this cheese! It's so milky and holey.'"

At the end of the play session, Ms. Abby shows David and Nadine the text she has written and reads the sentences aloud to them. David smiles and laughs as Ms. Abby reads, while Nadine stares at the paper with serious intensity. Later, when Ms. Abby invites the two children to share the story with the class, Nadine surprises Ms. Abby by holding the page and "reading" the story out loud to the class. Although it is clear that Nadine is reciting the words from memory, rather than decoding the text on the paper, this moment demonstrates a significant milestone in Nadine's development as a reader and writer. Nadine's creativity during dramatic play and her ability to remember specific words and phrases from the play session suggest that Nadine has the potential for advanced achievement in the areas of language and literacy.

Grouping Children

Teachers can be intentional about the way children will learn from each other by facilitating how children are paired or grouped together. By placing children in close proximity to each other, giving them a shared task to complete and assigning them specific roles, we are making powerful connections and providing learning opportunities both for the exceptionally bright children and for the rest of the children in the class. Group sizes range from large to small, from whole class to small groups, to triads and pairs. Decisions about the composition of a group should be made to balance both the needs of the group, for safe supervision and classroom management, and the individual needs of each child.

There is a growing body of evidence that children benefit from learning in mixed-age groups. The structure of many early childhood programs, in which children stay in the same classroom for two years, from age three to age five, is intentionally designed to increase the opportunities for social learning and to deepen the complexity of the connections made between children. The younger children, or those who are less mature cognitively or developmentally, gain from the exposure to older or more advanced children. The diversity of ability and knowledge in

Building a model of a beehive is an example of a collaborative project among children with a common interest and mixed ability levels.

a mixed-age group creates a rich and complex learning environment that goes beyond modeling and imitation and leads to the internalization of new understandings for children at all levels (Katz 1995; Gaustad 1997). The implication for our work with exceptionally bright children is that every child should have an opportunity to interact in groups with children who are both more advanced and less advanced than they are. Sometimes this will mean seeking out older, school-age children to partner with exceptionally bright preschool children. If your early childhood program does not serve older children, other options might include recruiting preteen volunteers or family members, such as older siblings, to visit and assist in your classroom.

Grouping children within a classroom according to ability is a practice that has some benefits to children, as long as the group membership is flexible (Hoffman 2002). Flexibility means the group assignments are temporary and that children are continually assessed and reassigned to groups as their abilities develop. Suppose a teacher divides her preschool class into three groups according to children's ability to write their names. The green group includes children who are able to write their names independently. The orange group includes children who are able to write one or two letters in their names. The blue group includes children who are just starting to learn to write their names. Although the teacher uses colors to label the groups, it won't take long for the children (and parents) to figure out which group is more advanced. If the teacher maintains these group assignments for just a few writing lessons, the children will likely benefit from the individualized, targeted experiences. But if the group assignments remain static over time, the children in the blue group (and their parents) may begin to develop a sense that they are behind, and all the children will lose the opportunities to learn from each other in a diverse learning community. Also, flexible grouping is an instructional practice that can be difficult for teachers to maintain because it requires frequent assessments and reconfigurations of the groups. If the groupings are not truly flexible, children will best benefit from being part of a group, triad, or pair that is formed based on other factors besides ability, for example, shared interests, learning styles, and similar or complementary temperaments or personalities.

Putting It All Together

Here's a story of one teacher's experience in finding a way to challenge an exceptionally bright child who has advanced knowledge and understanding of a specific topic. Sonya, a pre-K teacher, employs all three strategies—differentiation, conversation, and connection—to challenge an exceptionally bright child, Derek.

Four-year-old Derek loves trains. He's not just interested in trains, he is a complete train fanatic. He knows the difference between passenger cars and freight cars, and he can describe in detail the different kinds of cars in each category. According to Derek, the types of passenger cars are standard coaches, dining cars, sleeping cars, and baggage cars. Among the freight cars are boxcars, center beam cars, double stack cars, hoppers, refrigerator cars, and gondola cars.

Derek's teacher, Sonya, recognizes Derek's intense curiosity about trains and is eager to connect with him and support his interest. During her break time she goes through the school's storage closets looking for any extra sets of toy trains for Derek to play with. She finds a set of toy train cars and wooden tracks and eagerly presents the items to Derek after naptime. At first, Derek seems eager to play with the trains and he sits on the floor with the tub of toys, carefully removing each item. But a few minutes later, Sonya looks over as Derek kicks the box, bursts into tears, and says, "This train is no good! It's all wrong! There's no caboose; there's no hoppers or gondolas or any baggage cars! This is a stupid, stupid, stupid train!"

Sonya doesn't know how to respond. She feels frustrated that she went to so much trouble to find a train set for Derek, but now he's more upset than ever. She doesn't have any school funds to purchase additional toys for the classroom—and train sets that are as detailed and as accurate as Derek seems to be demanding cost a fortune. What can she do? And why can't Derek just make do with the perfectly good ordinary toys like the other children in the class?

Sonya realizes that she doesn't need to buy any new toys for Derek, but she does need to find ways not only to recognize and support Derek's advanced knowledge and vocabulary but also to challenge him to build on his understandings and grow even more. Some teachers might be tempted to steer Derek away from trains and in the direction of another topic, and help him build the same level of detailed knowledge in other areas, but clearly Derek loves trains and this is a special passion for him, one that could possibly last for his entire life and influence his career choices.

After some reading, reflection, and outside consultation with other professionals and mentors, Sonya makes a plan. First, she makes an effort to document what Derek already knows about trains. She says to Derek, "Tell me what you know about trains and I'll write it down." Derek relishes the opportunity to name the different kinds of trains he knows and loves. As he speaks, she asks follow-up questions such as, "How do you know a train car is a freight car and not a passenger car?" Over the next few weeks she uses a few spare minutes here and there to sit with Derek and take dictation, interview him, and read train books to him. She makes copies of diagrams and illustrations of trains from train books that she checks out from the adult nonfiction section of the library; then she sits with Derek and asks him to point to and name everything he sees in the diagrams. She writes down the words and labels that he dictates to her.

Together Sonya and Derek collect this information in a binder that they begin referring to as "Derek's Train Book." When Sonya begins to gain some confidence that she has a pretty good idea of what Derek knows about trains, she asks herself two questions: "How can I challenge Derek to extend what he knows about trains, to go further and learn more new information?" and "How can I help Derek deepen his understanding that he already has gained, and think about what he already knows in new ways?"

The first question is easier to answer. Sonya brings in a variety of train books from the library and presents them to Derek. After they look at them together and Derek spends some time with them on his own, Sonya notices that Derek is very excited about photos of the high-speed Eurostar trains that run through the Channel Tunnel between England and France. This will be a new area of knowledge for Derek to explore.

Sonya also wants to help Derek deepen his understanding of trains so he is not simply adding new words to his vocabulary but also thinking about the mechanics, physics, and engineering of train travel in ways he may have never considered before. To do this, Sonya returns to the train set that Derek had rejected earlier. She says to him, "I know this toy train is not like a real train, but we can use it to figure things out about the Eurostar. Let's take the toy train out to the sandbox during outdoor playtime and see if we can figure out a way to build a tunnel that the train can travel through." As they head out to the playground, Derek jumps and spins with joy, more excited than Sonya has ever seen him before.

Sonya has used several different successful strategies, all involving differentiation and conversation, to extend and deepen Derek's knowledge, skills, and abilities. But Sonya knows she has another important responsibility and opportunity here, to connect Derek to other children in the classroom. Sonya has observed that while Derek has advanced cognitive and verbal abilities, he has a very difficult time making friends with other children in the pre-K classroom. Most of the other children are not interested in trains to the same extent as Derek, and they quickly grow tired of Derek's insistence that trains are the center of every conversation. Derek spends most of his time at school playing alone and sitting and looking at train books. During outdoor play he can often be seen walking alone, talking to himself, lost in his own traincentric fantasy world.

Sonya's idea to invite Derek to take the toy trains outside to the sandbox is a great opportunity to try to encourage Derek to interact with other children. She knows that the sandbox is a popular spot on the playground and that Derek's tunnel project will bring him into closer proximity with other children. For now, that is progress for Derek, and she does not force him to include other children in digging his tunnel.

But soon enough, as Derek begins experimenting with digging a sand tunnel that will be strong enough for a toy train to travel through it, other children notice what Derek is doing and ask to be a part of it. Derek is not yet ready to negotiate and lead a group project on his own. Sonya plays the part of facilitator and gives each child a very specific role in the project. One child fetches the water to wet the sand, another is in charge of a small spoon that Derek has decided is the right size to scrape away at the walls of the tunnel. Sonya encourages the other children to ask Derek questions about the tunnel and the Eurostar train that inspired the project. After the class goes back indoors, during circle time, Sonya asks Derek to show the class photos of the Eurostar train and the Channel Tunnel.

Over the next few weeks, interest in trains catches on and soon the whole class wants to learn more about trains. Derek needs Sonya's support and guidance in his social interactions with other children, but he is making great strides, both cognitively and socially. And all the children in the class are benefiting, growing, and learning from the train project. Sonya is pleased to discover that the time and effort she put into working individually with Derek have paid off in her ability to teach and guide the entire class.

Chapter 6

Classroom Strategies for the Early Reader

The Many Faces of Advanced Language and Literacy Skills

An exceptionally bright child with advanced ability in the areas of language and literacy may be easy to recognize. A four-year-old who can accurately sight-read street signs and book titles is clearly advanced. A three-year-old who writes a letter to his mother, listing the reasons she should buy him a new Transformers toy, is also obviously quite advanced for his age, even if his spelling and sentence structure are still muddled. But other exceptionally bright children may have advanced literacy and language skills that are harder to recognize. Some examples could be the child with a sophisticated sense of humor and a broad repertoire of bizarre knock-knock jokes, or the child who makes up original songs to perform for her friends and family.

Whether children demonstrate their talents in traditional ways or in more unexpected manners, the three primary strategies of differentiation, conversation, and connection are effective responses. Differentiation occurs when we create a literacy-rich classroom environment and choose books at the appropriate level to engage and challenge children with advanced reading skills. Conversation plays an essential role in how we support the development of specific reading and writing skills. And connection is especially relevant in the process of encouraging children to create, write, and perform their own stories.

Early Readers/Natural Readers

In Harper Lee's novel, *To Kill a Mockingbird*, the character Jean Louise, also known as "Scout," learns to read at a very young age by following along as her father, Atticus Finch, reads aloud from the newspaper each evening. In chapter 2 of the novel, Scout reflects, "I could not remember when the lines above Atticus's moving finger separated into words, but I had stared at them all the evenings in my memory, listening to the news of the day . . . anything Atticus happened to be reading when I crawled into his lap every night. Until I feared I would lose it, I never loved to read. One does not love breathing."

For Scout, as for many young children with an exceptional talent for language and literacy, learning to read is a natural, fluid process that happens even before formal reading instruction begins. Books and stories play an important role in every child's learning experience, but for exceptionally bright children, books often become their best friends. Supporting advanced readers' interest in books and stories helps them develop the skills, both academic and social, that they will need to navigate the challenges they will face later in life. Advanced young readers, especially those who learn to read spontaneously and easily, are at risk of becoming bored and frustrated in a general preschool or pre-K classroom. For these children, the teacher's role is not so much to teach specific skills through direct instruction as it is to enhance and nurture the children's love of reading by helping them find books that will continue to challenge and entertain them. Children who experience learning to read as a natural process will also benefit from having conversations about what they've read, thereby learning to reflect on and think critically about the content of what they've read as well as to articulate the strategies they use in the mechanics of reading.

Keep in mind that the fact that some very young children, even as young as three or four, are able to read fluently doesn't mean that all children should be pushed to learn to read as early as possible. There's no research to support the idea that children who learn to read early are going to be more successful in school. And pressuring children to read before they are ready can cause more harm than good. By the same measure, care must be taken not to push children who are advanced readers to develop other skills or interests that are not meaningful to them. But for those few children who have an exceptional talent for reading, special care must be taken by their teachers and caregivers to ensure that they don't become bored and frustrated in their preschool or pre-K classrooms.

The Importance of a Literacy-Rich Environment

Creating a literacy-rich classroom is important for exceptionally bright children, as it is for all young children. The classroom environment is also the first place to look when thinking about how to differentiate language and literacy experiences for children at different levels of ability and interest. A literacy-rich environment is a place where children have a variety of opportunities to use language and engage with print by listening, reading, speaking, writing, and observing print all around them. This kind of environment offers children easy access to books and materials that interest them. This is especially important for exceptionally bright children because it allows them to make free choices about how and what to read and write.

A checklist for a literacy-rich environment would include:

Books
- ✓ books freely available for children to enjoy individually or in groups
- ✓ books on a variety of topics, not just those related to the current curriculum theme
- ✓ books at a range of reading levels, including picture books, chapter books, magazines, and teacher- or child-made books

Examples of the print in the environment
- ✓ signs and labels on walls and bulletin boards
- ✓ children's stories and ideas on display throughout the classroom
- ✓ reference materials, such as lists, recipes, and maps

Writing and drawing materials
- ✓ plenty of paper of different types and sizes, with lines and without
- ✓ a variety of writing utensils, including pencils, pens, markers, and crayons
- ✓ stencils, alphabet charts, and other resources children can refer to as they write letters and words
- ✓ a children's picture dictionary, such as *Scholastic Children's Dictionary*

Choosing the Right Book for the Right Child

Young children who are able to decode text and read independently need support and assistance from parents and teachers to find reading material that will challenge them and continue to expand their skills as readers and as learners.

At the same time they need books that are also appropriate for their age and emotional development.

Reading Levels

Many children's books, especially those used in school reading programs, have been evaluated for reading level, and often the reading level appears on the cover or title page. Matching the ideal reading level to the reader can be a confusing process because the systems for determining and labeling these levels differ from publisher to publisher. Some leveling systems correspond to grade levels, whereas others correlate to milestones in reading ability. A text that one publisher labels "easy" may be much more challenging to read than another publisher's version of "easy." It may be helpful to go to the children's section of your local library and spend a few minutes looking at books from a single publisher, such as an early reader series, and become familiar with how, in general, the text in a lower-level book varies from the text in a higher-level book. You will probably notice that the lower-level books use a larger font and have fewer words and sentences per page than the higher-level books. Also, the lower-level books tend to have shorter words and shorter sentences than the higher-level books.

For children who are reading at a level far beyond their chronological age and who are driven to read by their passion for books or for a particular topic, grade-level correlations may not have much relevance. For example, books labeled for beginning readers in kindergarten and first grade may seem like a logical choice for preschool children who are reading early. It's just the next step up the ladder in reading development. But these easy readers may actually be too easy, because they are often written especially for children who are struggling to decode words, to sound them out phonetically. Exceptionally bright children who have taught themselves to read often do not need help decoding. They have already cracked the code.

One common practice for determining if the reading level of a specific book is right for a given child is the "five finger rule." Have the child choose a page in the middle of the book and read one page, preferably a page that seems to have an average amount of text compared with other pages of the book. Have the child make a fist when she starts reading. When she comes to a word she doesn't know she should put up her thumb. If she finds another, she puts up one finger, and so on. If the child gets to the end of the page and hasn't raised any fingers, the book may be too easy for her. If she has raised two or three fingers the book probably offers the ideal level of reading challenge. But if she's raised all five fingers, the book is likely to be too challenging.

Subject Matter

For children who are advanced readers, the key to selecting a captivating book is often the book's subject rather than its reading level. A book on a fascinating subject, with appealing illustrations, may be a good fit for a particular child regardless of the level of the text. A four-year-old child who loves cats and enjoys books about magic might be motivated to pick up Ursula Le Guin's Catwings series, even though the reading level might be a bit beyond his current abilities. A child may be more willing and motivated to experiment with new reading strategies, to sound out difficult words, to use a dictionary, or to seek adult assistance when the subject of the book he wants to read is especially appealing.

Keep in mind that even though young children with advanced reading skills may have the ability to read quite advanced books, that does not necessarily mean those books are good choices for them. Many books that might technically be at the level of an exceptionally bright early reader are beyond a child's maturity level in terms of the subject and the content. A five-year-old may have the exceptional reading skills that would allow her to read a young adult book like *The Hunger Games* by Suzanne Collins, but she does not have the intellectual and emotional maturity to be able to understand and process the sociopolitical and emotional themes, much less the violence, presented in the book. When in doubt, consult the librarian or media specialist in your school or at your local library for advice about selecting books for a specific young reader. Here are some suggested books for advanced young readers:

Picture books. Even after children learn to read with fluency, they still enjoy and benefit from reading picture books. Children who are advanced readers may enjoy more complex picture book stories such as the beautifully illustrated books by Chris Van Allsburg, author of *Jumanji*. Young children with advanced language skills may also enjoy wordless picture books, such as David Wiesner's *Flotsam* or Barbara Lehman's *The Red Book*. With these books, they can be encouraged to tell their own stories.

Nonfiction and reference books. Exceptionally bright young children often develop a passionate interest in a specific topic and will enjoy exploring books on that topic even if they are not able to read all the text. Children's librarians are often good sources for recommendations of nonfiction children's books. One frequently recommended option for nonfiction books are those by DK Publishing. The DK Eyewitness series includes books on a variety of nonfiction topics that include vivid and detailed photographs. Another option are books by Picture Window Books, publisher of nonfiction books for young children, such as the Amazing Science series. Exceptionally bright young children may also enjoy exploring traditional reference books, such as illustrated encyclopedias and dictionaries.

Chapter books. Children who are able to read independently with some fluency, which means they do not have to stop and sound out words very often, might be interested in reading short chapter books. Chapter books are usually not included in most preschool and pre-K class libraries, so teachers must make the effort to seek these out and have them available on classroom bookshelves. Some recommended chapter books include the Magic Tree House series by Mary Pope Osborne and the Junie B. Jones series by Barbara Park.

Comic books and graphic novels. Child-friendly comic books and graphic novels, such as the delightful Owly series by Andy Runton and the Babymouse series by Jennifer and Matthew Holm, are fun choices for early readers.

Funny books. Joke books and silly books, such as the Elephant and Piggie easy reader series by Mo Willems, are especially good choices for advanced but reluctant readers.

Suggested Strategies for Teaching Advanced Readers

When we set up a reading corner and stock the shelves with wonderful books, we can do more than just sit back and hope the children will read. We can engage children in conversations and experiences that move them from passive to active engagement with print (Bennett-Armistead, Duke, and Moses 2005). This means inviting and directing children to use language, listening, writing, and reading for authentic purposes that have real meaning in their lives. As described in chapter 4, engaging children in meaningful conversations, in this case about books, text, and symbols, is one of the three core strategies, the braided thread, for challenging exceptionally bright children.

Authentic Uses of Language and Literacy

What matters most to young children? The two topics that immediately come to mind are their families and their play. Children's experiences with reading and writing will be meaningful to them when we connect these experiences with their family relationships or integrate these experiences into their pretend play. The following list includes ideas for actions that can be used to connect children to their families or can be included as part of pretend play. Any of these suggestions can be used as the basis of a conversation or activity that develops and challenges children's language and literacy skills:

- Ask a question.
- Develop a survey.
- Write in a journal.
- Label a drawing.
- Tell a story.
- Draw a map.
- Make a list.
- Read to a friend.
- Listen to a story.
- Create a secret code.
- Write a letter.
- Send an e-mail.

Author Studies

If an exceptionally bright child develops a passionate interest in a specific book or series of books, one way to explore that interest is to help the child create an author study. An author study might include looking at an author's website and learning about his or her life and reading other books written by the same author. Reading multiple books by the same author can help develop children's critical-thinking skills because they will be able to think about the author's body of work rather than looking at each book in isolation. Children can talk, dictate, or write their own book reviews, evaluating and comparing books using a variety of criteria. Teachers can prompt children to critique the books by asking questions along the lines of, "In your opinion, which book was the most creative?" or "Which book was the best? Why do you think so?"

Writing a letter or e-mail message to an author is, in itself, an advanced literacy activity, and children are likely to be thrilled and inspired if the author writes them back. Kate DiCamillo, author of picture books, chapter books, and novels for children, such as the humorous Mercy Watson early-reader series, is known to respond to each of her fan letters with a handwritten postcard. Other prolific authors who could be the subject of an author study include Grace Lin, Eric Carle, Arthur Dorros, Mo Willems, Faith Ringgold, Mem Fox, and Jan Brett.

Dictation and Dramatization

Children who are advanced readers sometimes feel isolated from their peers in the general classroom. Engaging all children in story dictation and story acting

> "Once upon a time there lived a pirate named Captain Flag He loved to sail away to where there was lots and lots of treasure."

Example of a dictated story.

(dramatization) is a great way to create a sense of community while still providing opportunities for early readers to advance their language and literacy skills. Both the dictation process and the dramatization process allow exceptionally bright children to go deeper into the creative process of telling and writing stories and to develop more sophisticated and complex uses of language. Story dictation and dramatization are both classroom activities that can be used to encourage partnerships and teamwork among the children. As described in chapter 5, creating connections between children is one of the most important strategies for challenging exceptionally bright children. Story dictation may begin as a one-on-one activity but lends itself well to collaboration and sharing. The term "story dictation" refers to what happens when a child tells a story (or offers a narrative description of an event or person) and an adult or an older child writes down the child's words, exactly as the child has spoken them. The finished stories can then be bound in a book, posted on a bulletin board, or read aloud and dramatized.

Story dictation is a valuable part of any early childhood setting because it fosters children's language, literacy, social, and emotional development. Acting out the stories in small groups is an important opportunity for children to share their stories with others and build friendships. All the children benefit from these practices, but children who are early readers are particularly challenged and supported as they develop new language and literacy skills.

With a little practice, some children will create stories that are wholly original and fascinating in their complexity; for example, this one:

Once upon a time there was a princess that got confused all the time. And her father, the king, thought that she did it for fun. And he sent her to her room. And she jumped out the window. The king got so mad that he made her sleep in the dungeon for one night. And next morning he said to himself, "What has gotten into that girl?" Then he said, "What's wrong with you?" to the princess. On her third birthday the king said, "Maybe I should get you a copy of a book called Never Forget Things and that will teach you not to forget." But she kept on forgetting even though he got her the book. One day she said, "Maybe we should go fishing," but she caught no fish and the king caught four fish. And the princess could do beautiful embroidery but she couldn't fish. She found a prince and they married and the princess never forgetted again. They went camping and they had a good time. They went swimming with their beach ball. They found a robin's nest with eggs in it. They saw a shooting star at night.

To learn more about story dictation, see my book *Story Dictation: A Guide for Early Childhood Professionals* (available from Redleaf Press).

Bringing Stories to Life

One of the best ways to build on and share stories in your classroom is to have the children act them out or dramatize them. Bringing stories to life is a great way to build a sense of community and connect children to each other, a process that is especially important for exceptionally bright children who may feel socially isolated from their peers and yet have the ability to serve as great role models. Creating and acting out stories is also an example of social learning, as described in chapter 5, when children interact with each other at various levels of ability. The process of acting out stories also deepens children's understanding of the elements of a story and, in turn, improves their ability to tell or write good stories. For example, when children are acting out a story they will often add dialogue that was not included in the dictated story. Teachers can encourage children to return to their stories and revise them by adding dialogue. Children with advanced language and literacy skills may be especially responsive to these suggestions.

In most early childhood settings, the dramatization of stories would best take place during large-group or circle time. The teacher gathers the children together and the author of a story is invited to stand before the group while the teacher reads the story aloud. Then the roles in the story are assigned to specific children and the teacher reads the story again, this time pausing after each sentence or action to allow the children to use gestures or movements to demonstrate the events and actions in the story. There is no rehearsal necessary and the teacher serves as a stage manager, making gentle suggestions to the actors for ways they can show what is happening in the story.

Teachers who make the acting out of dictated stories a regular part of their classroom routine tell me that dramatizing stories is very satisfying for the children and something the whole class eagerly anticipates. Teachers frequently comment that children who tend to become restless and disruptive during traditional story time often become engaged and cooperative when they are given the opportunity to act out their own stories or the stories of their friends. The opportunity to dramatize stories also seems to motivate children to dictate stories and develop more exciting and interesting plots and characters.

Advanced, Yet Reluctant

The term "reluctant reader" is often used to describe children who have very little interest in books. Often older children, such as those in the primary grades who are struggling to develop reading skills, are reluctant readers. What may be surprising, however, is that some children with advanced language and literacy skills may also be reluctant to read. In fact, you may become aware of a child's exceptional gifts for reading only by accident, when the child happens to correctly read a sign or list in the environment that was intended only for adults.

Advanced readers who resist picking up a book may do so for a variety of reasons. They may be bored with the reading materials they've encountered so far, and need books that are more difficult to read and that address more complex subjects or stories. Or they might feel anxious about reading because the adults in their lives have recognized their advanced skills, and those adults' enthusiasm and praise have created feelings of pressure in the children to perform and achieve. The task of the teacher is to gently balance encouragement with opportunity, taking care not to push children while still presenting multiple opportunities to engage with print. Creating a literacy-rich environment, matching the right book to the right child, and engaging children in story dictation are just some of the strategies that might help entice a reluctant reader of any ability level to begin to love reading.

Reading Aloud to Children Still Matters

Just because a child has already learned to read doesn't mean that the adults in her life should stop reading to her. There is a wealth of research to support the idea that reading aloud to children is positively correlated with higher achievement at any level, regardless of when the child begins to read independently (Trelease 1995; Wadsworth 2008). All children benefit from hearing stories read aloud, and all children should have daily opportunities to enjoy the books they love with their families and friends.

Exceptionally bright children often benefit from a wider variety of read-aloud books than children with normal cognitive development. For example, in many high-quality early childhood classrooms teachers have a collection of "go to" classic picture books that they read frequently, such as *Caps for Sale* by Esphyr Slobodkina. Although exceptionally bright children also enjoy these books, their ability to learn quickly and their tendency to seek novel experiences mean that they may not enjoy the repetition of these books as much as other children. Challenging these children means finding new and more advanced books to read aloud in small groups and one-on-one.

Classroom Strategies for the Advanced Mathematician

Chapter 7

Recognizing Advanced Math Skills

How do we know if a young child is exceptionally bright in the area of math when the young children in our classrooms are not yet taking math exams and solving equations? What does math talent look like in very young children? What behaviors might we see that indicate a special talent for mathematics? For most people, the word "mathematics" brings to mind numbers and counting. Even in the field of early childhood education, we often think of the acquisition of simple arithmetic skills as the first step in learning to do math. Numbers and counting tend to be the focus of most preschool math activities and curriculum planning. Numbers are also the focus of most state early learning math standards across the nation. For example, in the *Pre-Kindergarten: Pennsylvania Learning Standards for Early Childhood* (Pennsylvania Department of Education and Department of Public Welfare 2009), the first standards in the category of "Mathematical Thinking" include:

- rote (learned through repetition) count to twenty
- count up to ten objects using one-to-one correspondence
- name numerals to ten

Most other states' math standards begin similarly, pointing to a general consensus that being good at math in the early years means being able to count to twenty and beyond. However, math is much more than counting. A very young child's advanced math skills may be demonstrated in ways that are not traditionally associated with numbers and counting. Instead of performing familiar functions like counting, adding, and subtracting, young children with truly advanced abilities in mathematical thinking are more likely to excel at creative, analytical thinking that involves some of these problem-solving processes:

- sorting
- measuring
- comparing
- organizing
- ordering
- reasoning
- estimating
- predicting

Young children who are exceptionally bright in the area of math may also behave in ways that show they are thinking not only about numbers but also about groups, quantities, shapes, distances, and time, and they do so in flexible, creative, complex, and unconventional ways. For example, a child with a talent for math may be less likely to express her knowledge using the vocabulary of arithmetic (*Two plus two equals four*) and more likely to notice with delight how many triangles can be found in the illustrations on a box of cereal.

This is not to say that children with exceptional math skills are not interested in numbers and counting. Some clearly are. Many have an intense fascination with the tools that employ numbers, such as phones, calendars, rulers, thermometers, and calculators. And some do exhibit their competency in traditional ways, such as counting to one hundred and beyond, surpassing the basic arithmetic standards for their age group.

Though very few research studies measure early math aptitude in very young children, an article in the *Journal for the Education of the Gifted* titled "Parents' Observations of Math-Precocious Preschoolers" (Pletan et al. 1995) describes some of the interesting behaviors parents reported as the first noticeable clues that their children were exceptionally bright in the area of math. Included in the reports were these examples:

- a child who could identify all the states by shape alone and place them in a puzzle accurately without using any outline clues
- a child who loved to organize and reorganize complex collections of things, such as baseball cards, using different sorting criteria, for example, colors of the uniforms, ages of the players, and batting averages
- a child who could memorize detailed patterns, such as the numbers and letters on license plates viewed on a long car trip
- a child who would rather play with a stopwatch than any toy
- a child who was fascinated by the differences between odd and even numbers
- a child who became interested in written music and how the notes and rests divide each measure

If young children demonstrate similar behaviors that indicate advanced abilities in mathematical thinking or have already mastered early learning goals and objectives in the area of math, it is clear that they will benefit from experiences that will continue to challenge and expand their math skills and their understanding of the world of mathematics.

Foundational Math Skills

As we think about how to challenge children who are exceptionally bright in the area of math, we may be tempted to think only about how to accelerate their math skills to a higher level, as measured by academic grade. Our first impulse may be to introduce kindergarten, first-, or second-grade math materials such as addition and subtraction flash cards. My experience in developing math enrichment courses for young bright children is that they will benefit more from deepening the foundations of their math understanding than from accelerating the math content to higher grade levels.

This deepening of understanding is an important part of the concept of "foundational mathematics" utilized by the Erikson Institute's Early Mathematics Education Project (http://earlymath.erikson.edu). This groundbreaking project provides professional development to preschool and kindergarten teachers in Chicago Public Schools, and the Erikson Institute also serves as host of the International Symposium on Early Mathematics Education. The Early Mathematics Education Project uses the term foundational mathematics to describe the mathematical thinking that all young children need to develop in order to be well prepared to advance their math skills and knowledge in the primary grades.

Foundational mathematics emphasizes the "big ideas" that young children can explore to build the foundations for knowledge and thinking in the five content strands named by the National Council of Teachers of Mathematics (accessed 2012):

- number and operations
- algebra
- geometry
- measurement
- data analysis and probability

"Big Ideas" in the Early Childhood Classroom

For early childhood professionals with little training or experience in teaching mathematics, some of these content strands may sound intimidating. Algebra and geometry, for example, are subjects usually taught in middle school or high school. It may be surprising to learn, then, that the seeds of these content strands can be planted and explored as big ideas in an early childhood curriculum. Before addressing how to support advanced mathematicians, it's important to define each strand to know what it often looks like in early childhood.

Number and Operations

This content strand is probably most familiar to early childhood professionals. When children learn the names of numbers, when they count by rote, and when they begin to use one-to-one correspondence to count, they are learning the foundations of number and operations. Big ideas related to number and operations include the idea that any set, or group, contains a certain quantity of elements. This is also called the concept of cardinality. When children learn to answer questions that begin with "How many . . . ," they are developing their understanding of this concept. Another important, yet more advanced, big idea related to number and operations is the understanding that the numeral system we use most often is a "base ten" system, which means essentially that every digit in a given number has a position and each position farther to the left is ten times larger than the one to the right of it. In a base ten system, a two-digit number has a "ones" column and a "tens" column. When children learn to count by tens, whether they are using dimes or Unifix cubes or simply counting in their heads, they are developing their understanding of a base ten system.

Algebra

Algebra is a branch of mathematics that deals with the relationships between and among numeric values. Unknown values are represented as symbols, for example, the letter x in the following statements:

$$1 + x = 3$$
$$x = 3 - 1$$
$$3 - x = 1$$

This concept that mathematical quantities and relationships can be represented by symbols is one of the big ideas underlying algebraic thinking. Another big idea is the concept that groups can be sorted in more than one way. A group of six buttons can be sorted into two piles of three or three piles of two. Complexity is added to the exercise when young children sort larger groups of buttons into piles, arranging and rearranging the piles based on different characteristics, such as color, size, or shape. The sorting process invites children to explore and develop a system of relationships between the specified members of a set.

Geometry

Geometry is the branch of mathematics that deals with the properties and relationships of lines, points, angles, and figures in space. The big ideas under the category of geometry include not just the names of shapes but the identification of the characteristics of shapes and the understanding of the relationships between shapes. For example, when children discover that two triangles can be put together to make a square, they are exploring the big idea that shapes can be combined to make new shapes. Learning to notice and talk about the characteristics of shapes and solving problems using blocks or puzzle pieces are early childhood experiences that lay the foundation for geometry.

Measurement

Measuring is one of the ways math is frequently used in ordinary daily experiences. We measure time with clocks, we measure ingredients with cups and spoons, and we measure the height of children by marking lines on a doorframe and exclaiming, "My, how big you've grown!" The big ideas under the category of measurement include the concepts of standard and nonstandard units of measurement. Standard units of measurement include inches, minutes, and quarts, while a nonstandard unit of measurement could be practically anything. The length of a sandbox could be measured by a row of buckets and its width measured by laying shovels end to end. In this case, the buckets and the shovels are the nonstandard units. When children measure and compare, they are learning the foundation of measurement skills that will serve them for the rest of their lives, regardless of the career path they choose.

Data Analysis

One of the biggest big ideas behind data analysis is the understanding that solving math problems and answering math questions almost always involves collecting and organizing data, or facts. Suppose the children in a preschool class are wondering how many birds visit the school's bird feeder each day. When they keep a tally of how many birds they see over the course of a day, they are engaging in data collection. Later, the teacher may help the children count the tally and make a chart showing their findings. This is data analysis. Other big ideas in the category of data analysis include the concepts of graphing and mapping. When children learn to write down math information using numerals or other symbol systems, like the tally marks, they are developing a foundation for understanding data analysis that they can build upon in later, more sophisticated work, such as statistics.

Math and the Braided Thread

The braided thread of important classroom strategies (differentiation, conversation, and connection) is just as relevant to math instruction as it is for language and literacy. Differentiation allows teachers to create challenging math experiences for all the children in the class. Conversation provides opportunities for children to explain their thinking about math, to ask and answer questions, and to reflect on their problem-solving strategies. And teachers can use connection strategies to help children learn from each other. These strategies support all learners but can be especially effective tools for challenging exceptionally bright mathematicians.

Differentiation of the Math Curriculum

Challenging children with advanced mathematical ability requires differentiation. As discussed in chapter 3, differentiation can be accomplished in a variety of ways: by adjusting the way you teach, by making changes in the classroom environment, and by differentiating your curriculum plans, adding activities and experiences that will meet the individual needs of the exceptionally bright children in the group. In the area of math, adjusting the way you teach may mean accelerating the pace of instruction and the complexity of curriculum content to ensure that the exceptionally bright children are consistently challenged with new math concepts. For example, regarding the content strand of numbers and operations, you may be accustomed to developing activities and games that teach children to count up to ten, using one-to-one correspondence. You may even be prepared to expand and scaffold those experiences over the course of the school year to include counting to twenty. An exceptionally bright child may progress through these activities very quickly. He may be ready to count beyond twenty by early October. What next? How will you maintain an accelerated pace of instruction for the rest of the school year? Challenging this child may mean not only adjusting the activities and games so he has opportunities to count to much higher numbers but also introducing more complex counting methods, such as skip counting, which means counting by fives or tens. Thinking about and researching the big ideas in each math content strand will help you remember that math can be much more complex and interesting than just rote counting and one-to-one correspondence. The following are some ideas to get you started.

Games and Manipulatives

Differentiating by making changes to the classroom environment may mean adding games and manipulatives that have been created for slightly older children. Some materials I recommend for use with exceptionally bright young children include:

- Board games: Children learn skills like prediction and estimation by playing games like Connect 4, Guess Who?, Battleship, Blokus, and checkers.
- Open-ended game pieces: Children gain experience counting, adding, and subtracting by using cards, dice, spinners, and dominoes to create their own games.
- Geometry manipulatives: Children are exposed to geometry concepts by playing with items such as geoboards, parquetry blocks, tangrams, and pattern blocks.
- Puzzle books: Children acquire logical reasoning when playing paper-and-pencil games like tic-tac-toe and Sudoku.

Hands-On Curriculum

Another way to differentiate to meet the needs of exceptionally bright children is to increase the complexity and depth of the math curriculum in everyday activities. The study of geometry is an especially exciting avenue for very young mathematicians because the principles of geometry can so easily be explored through play. Because traditional preschool block play (with materials such as unit blocks, hollow blocks, or parquetry blocks) is so open-ended, there are ample opportunities to challenge exceptionally bright young children. The tactile, visual, and kinesthetic experience of playing with blocks exposes all children to geometric concepts, such as the properties of shapes. Many exceptionally bright children are ready to name and develop these geometric concepts.

Geometric Concepts to Explore through Play

A child who demonstrates advanced abilities or an unusual curiosity about math or shapes may benefit from some adult guidance in how to explore specific geometric principles.

The properties of shapes. Once children have mastered the identification of shapes, they can be challenged to learn more sophisticated concepts and vocabulary regarding the properties of shapes, for instance, symmetry and angles. These concepts can be introduced to children before, during, or after block and puzzle play through conversations, questions, modeling, or picture books.

Proportion. Children who are ready to think more deeply about shapes can also think about the proportions—relationships between shapes of different sizes. Rulers and other measuring tools can be used in combination with blocks to help children do this. For example, encourage children to document what they see and do with blocks through drawings and

Scale drawing.

tracings. Eventually, some children may be able to make their own scale drawings, such as in the example shown, in which a child has created a sketch of a house she made with pattern blocks. The drawing is exactly half the size of the block structure. With her teacher's assistance she has created a key that explains that one inch in the block structure is represented by half an inch in her drawing.

Coordinates. In geometry, coordinates are used to find locations on a grid. Children can be introduced to the concept of a grid by drawing or building with blocks on graph paper or on a grid of lines made with masking tape.

Dimension. Some exceptionally bright young children may be interested in thinking about the differences between two- and three-dimensional shapes. Again, teachers can use conversation and questions to introduce children to the term "dimension" and draw the children's attention to examples of images and objects that demonstrate these concepts. Using paper, pencils, and measuring tools in combination with block play gives children opportunities to compare and contrast two- and three-dimensional shapes.

Putting It into Words

Conversation, the second strategy in the braided thread for challenging exceptionally bright children, is an important way to challenge children to develop mathematical thinking and explain their problem-solving process. You've probably heard math teachers at the elementary, middle, and high school level urge their students to "show your work." Actually, even more valuable than showing is telling. Getting students to articulate their problem-solving process is often one of the primary goals in a gifted education classroom. This is also a worthy goal for an early childhood classroom where all the children are still early in the process of developing language. Asking children open-ended questions, as described in chapter 4, is just as important for math as it is in any other subject area.

Conversational dictation can be used to document children's mathematical thinking. Unlike story dictation, as described in chapter 6, conversational dictation involves writing down what children say during a spontaneous conversation. Suppose a pre-K teacher notices that four-year-old Matthew has removed all the wooden puzzle pieces from the frames of four different puzzles: a train puzzle, a car puzzle, a truck puzzle, and an airplane puzzle. Her first instinct is to urge Matthew to clean up the mess he has made! But she pauses and observes that Matthew is sorting and separating the puzzle pieces into piles. She grabs a notepad and pencil and approaches Matthew.

Teacher: Matthew, I'm interested in what you're doing with the puzzle pieces. Tell me about it.

Matthew: I'm just playing.

Teacher: It looks like fun. I see you moving that round piece and putting it in a pile. Why did you do that?

Matthew: Because it's a wheel.

Teacher: Yes, I see. The other pieces in that pile, are they all wheels?

Matthew:	Yeah. I want all the wheels together.
Teacher:	That's very interesting. I'd like to write down your words; is that okay with you? (Matthew shrugs and the teacher begins to write.) Let's see, you said, "I want all the wheels together." There, I wrote your words. Tell me more. Why do you want all the wheels together?
Matthew:	Because they're round. They roll and make everything go.
Teacher:	What are you doing now?
Matthew:	I'm stacking them up. If I get another one, I'll have six.
Teacher:	(still writing) You have six wheels?
Matthew:	It's not enough, though. Six is not enough.
Teacher:	Not enough for what?
Matthew:	To make it all go.
Teacher:	To make what go?
Matthew:	All of them. The car and the truck and the train and the plane. It's not enough.
Teacher:	Not enough?
Matthew:	(nodding) The car should have four and the truck four too. I don't know how many for the plane and the train.
Teacher:	Are you thinking about how many wheels a real car and truck have?
Matthew:	(nodding and pointing to the stack of puzzle pieces) I don't have enough.
Teacher:	Hmm. Maybe you're wondering why the number of wheels in your pile doesn't match the number of wheels on a real car and truck?
Matthew:	And plane too. And train too. Where are they? Where are all the wheels?
Teacher:	Do you think some wheels are missing?
Matthew:	(nodding) The puzzles are wrong.

By documenting her conversation with Matthew, using conversational dictation and note taking, the teacher now has a rich demonstration of the complexity of Matthew's analytical skills. Not only is Matthew using the puzzle pieces in an unconventional way by sorting pieces into piles according to attributes such as shape and function, but he is also demonstrating several levels of abstract thinking. He is seeing the puzzle pieces in at least four different ways: as individual shapes, as parts of a whole, as pieces of flat pictures, and as representations of real objects.

The documentation of this conversation can also be used to help Matthew reflect on his own thinking (metacognition) and make a plan for further learning and exploration. His teacher can read the dictated conversation back to Matthew and ask follow-up questions that promote reflection (*What do you still want to know about the puzzles or about the wheels?*). Perhaps Matthew wants to know why there aren't enough wheels. To answer that question, Matthew might decide to put all four puzzles back together again and then count the number of wheels represented in the images on the puzzles. As he thinks about why the flat images on the puzzles don't show all the wheels on the actual vehicles, this process will challenge Matthew to think critically about issues of perspective and dimension.

Making Connections: Math and Social Learning

The third strategy in the braided thread, connection, is based on the idea that learning is a social experience. This is certainly true for learning math. Children gain mathematical knowledge, skills, and ideas through conversations and interactions with both adults and other children. As described in chapter 5, children learn from the adults in their lives and they also learn a lot from each other. Even a child with very advanced mathematical abilities will gain new insights from interactions with other children, as long as these experiences are rich, meaningful, and complex. The way to develop these kinds of experiences is to capitalize on opportunities for children to use math in their daily experiences.

Using Math in Everyday Life
During each ordinary day in the lives of young children, the adults around them use math to communicate, solve problems, coordinate schedules, and conduct business. Children with a special talent or interest in math can be included in these tasks and given roles that will challenge them and help them understand math in the context of our everyday lives. Some of the roles children can play include:

- Cooking: figuring out how to double a cookie recipe to make two batches of cookies at once.
- Money: sorting and counting the coins that families have brought to school with their picture orders.

- Temperature: helping set the classroom thermostat for a warmer temperature (under close supervision, of course).
- Time: estimating how long it will take for everyone to have a turn using the classroom microscope.

Math in Picture Books

One strategy for challenging exceptionally bright children with new math concepts and ideas, especially for teachers and caregivers who are more comfortable with early literacy than with early math, is to use storybooks as a launching point for math conversations and math activities. Stories related to math content can be read and discussed in groups or one-on-one. Math-friendly picture books include *Actual Size* by Steve Jenkins and *Math Curse* by Jon Scieszka. Picture book authors who have focused their work on math-related topics include Tana Hoban, Mitsumasa Anno, and Stuart J. Murphy. A full list of recommended math books and resources appears in appendix A. Many of the books include ideas and explanations for parents and teachers about how to use the book for exploring math concepts.

Math-Friendly Technology

Hands-on play, manipulating blocks and other concrete objects, is the best way for young children to learn, regardless of their cognitive ability. While technology should never replace these traditional play experiences, some exceptionally bright children may benefit from playing challenging, creative, and interactive computer games. Beware of games marketed specifically as games for learning math. Many are simply flash cards in disguise and are intended to teach math facts and functions through repetitive practice. The kinds of multitouch mobile device applications or web-based activities that will fascinate exceptionally bright young children are ones created for entertainment that have some kind of engaging problem-solving component.

For example, the multitouch mobile device application Bubble Harp from Scott Snibbe Studio is an innovative application that combines drawing, animation, and geometry. The application responds to movements of the finger on a touch screen by creating polygons in patterns that resemble bubbles, honeycombs, spiderwebs, or fish scales. Young children will likely be fascinated by the shapes, movements, and patterns. Children can also be challenged to re-create their Bubble Harp patterns on paper or using blocks or string.

For additional guidance and ideas, read *Teaching in the Digital Age: Smart Tools for Age 3 to Grade 3* by Brian Puerling, which is based on the 2012 joint position statement on technology from the National Association for the Education of Young Children (NAEYC) and the Fred Rogers Center (FRC). Another great resource is the Technology in Early Childhood (TEC) Center of the Erikson Institute. The TEC Center website (www.teccenter.erikson .edu) provides information about the use of technology in early childhood classrooms. Both of these resources offer information for teaching children of all skill and ability levels, but many of the recommendations for children in kindergarten and the primary grades are appropriate for exceptionally bright preschool children.

Teacher as Math Role Model

Planning advanced math activities can be an intimidating task for those of us who don't have a strong background in math. If we don't feel confident in our own math abilities, it can be difficult to act as a positive role model for children. Often our insecurities about our own math skills are unfounded. For example, often girls and women receive messages from society, directly and indirectly, that they are inferior to boys and men when it comes to math. It is important that we resist this kind of bias. As professionals in the field of education, we must take responsibility for learning or reviewing the math concepts we need to understand in order to act as confident role models for the young children in our classrooms. When I began developing ideas for challenging block play activities for exceptionally bright young children, I found that my own knowledge of basic geometry concepts was pretty rusty. I used online resources to review math concepts I had studied in school many years ago. (A list of suggested resources for math review for adults is included in appendix A.) Once I felt more comfortable using math vocabulary and explaining math concepts, I found that I truly enjoyed having conversations with young children about math and felt more confident asking and answering questions. The process of reviewing my own math understanding helped to remind me that math is so much more than numbers; it can be a way of understanding the world around us.

Classroom Strategies for the Young Scientist

The Scientific Mind

Children who are exceptionally bright in the area of science are likely very observant, carefully watching all kinds of phenomena in the natural world. They notice how things grow or how our bodies work, and they look under lids or rocks, noting the diversity and intricacy of the world around them. They may demonstrate an intense and focused curiosity about certain things, such as the child who, on a class field trip to a farm, refuses to move away from the incubator, determined to stay and watch every detail of a chick hatching from an egg. Children with scientific minds may be extraordinarily curious about technology and mechanics, observing how things are built, how they work, and how to fix things that are broken.

Throughout history, many great scientists, including Marie Curie and Thomas Edison, have been remembered as demonstrating unusually intense levels of curiosity as young children. Albert Einstein often told the story of his fascination, at just four years old, with the workings of a magnetic compass. He felt that there had to be "something behind things, something deeply hidden" (American Institute of Physics 2004). Like Einstein, young children with an unusual aptitude for science are intense and curious observers. In addition to curiosity, some other personality traits you might see in children with an exceptional talent for science include:

- playfulness
- risk taking
- originality
- persistence
- independence

Braiding the Thread

In science, all three strategies for challenging bright children—differentiation, conversation, and connection—are truly woven and bound together. In fact, it's difficult to talk about them as separate strategies because the two examples of best practice discussed in this chapter—using the scientific method and inquiry-based learning to build on children's interests—require a continuous mix of all three strategies.

The Scientific Method

Regardless of what scientific topic captures the interest of the children in your class, you will be best equipped to challenge the exceptionally bright children if you structure your science-related curriculum using the scientific method. The scientific method is a standardized technique used in the field of science and science education for investigating scientific or natural phenomena and deepening our understanding of how the world works. The scientific method follows a sequence like this:

1. Ask a question.
2. Do preliminary research on the question.
3. Construct a hypothesis, which is a possible explanation as to how or why something occurs.
4. Conduct an experiment or make intentional observations that test the hypothesis or try to show it is wrong.
5. Analyze the data and draw a conclusion.
6. Communicate the results by presenting your findings to others.

It's important to note that if your results in step 5 don't show your hypothesis to be wrong, then you know it *could be* right. In the scientific realm, if enough experiments are done or observations made, and enough consistent results collected, then scientists conclude that a hypothesis is *likely to be* correct.

In a preschool or pre-K classroom, the scientific method might look like this:

1. **Ask a question.** One day on the playground a child asks, "Why doesn't the grass grow on the sidewalk?" The teacher *could* respond, "Because cement does not have the same nutrients as soil," or any number of logical, informed explanations. Instead, the teacher uses the question as a starting point for scientific exploration and replies, "That's a good question. I'm going to write it down. 'Why doesn't grass grow on the sidewalk?' Let's find out."

2. **Do preliminary research on the question.** With the teacher's support and facilitation, the child conducts some research by thinking about and compiling what she knows about seeds, sidewalks, and so on. She may also talk to adults, and look at books independently or with the help of an adult. Even picture books can be helpful. She learns that plants need soil, water, and sunshine to grow. She learns that many plants grow in garden soil that is dark brown in color, moist, and soft.

3. **Construct a hypothesis.** Now that the child has gathered some information, the teacher invites her to come up with her own idea that might answer the original question. The teacher states that the goal is to make a hypothesis and explains that a hypothesis is "a guess based on what we think could be a good explanation." He asks the child, "What's your guess? What is your hypothesis for why the grass does not grow on the sidewalk?" She replies, "Because the sidewalk is hard. The ground has to be soft to grow things." The teacher says, "That's an interesting idea. I'm going to write it down and post it on the wall where everyone can see it and think about it."

4. **Conduct an experiment that tests the hypothesis.** The teacher helps the child come up with a plan for testing the hypothesis. By this time, many other children in the class have become interested in the process and want to be part of the experiment. The children fill two pots, one with soil and one with a few chunks of hard cement. They sprinkle grass seeds across the top of each filled pot. They set the pots on a sunny windowsill and water the pots every morning. Each day the children draw pictures and

take photos of what they see in each pot. On the seventh day, the grass seeds in the soil begin to sprout.

5. **Analyze the data and draw a conclusion.** The teacher helps the children number all their drawings and photos and display them, in order, on a classroom wall. He invites them to study the data they have collected and draw a conclusion. "Do you think your guess, your hypothesis, was right? Does grass need something soft to grow?" The children decide the answer is probably yes. The hypothesis is likely to be correct.

6. **Communicate the results.** The teacher helps the children create a mural that demonstrates the entire process, from the question and initial research to the hypothesis to the experiment to the conclusion. Parents are invited to view the mural. The teacher follows up by asking the children, "What other questions do you have that haven't been answered?" One of the children asks, "What makes the sidewalk so hard?" This question will lead to further explorations and discovery.

In addition to curiosity and passive observation, children with an aptitude for scientific thinking have the capacity to draw conclusions and make predictions about what they observe. When teachers use the scientific method to explore ideas and questions, there are multiple opportunities for differentiation, conversation, and connection. For example, differentiation takes place because the scientific method is open ended enough to allow exceptionally bright children to ask even more complex questions than their peers ask, as well as to challenge them to think more deeply about the process, draw conclusions, and make predictions.

Drawing Conclusions

When we draw conclusions we are using information, facts, or ideas to determine other new information or ideas. A child may notice at the end of lunchtime that the bowl of carrots is still half full but the bowl of strawberries is almost empty and draw the conclusion that "kids like strawberries better than carrots." Sometimes young children, because they still have so much to learn about the world, draw conclusions that are inaccurate. Suppose a child sits on the playground, using his fingers to tear blades of grass into tiny pieces, and then looks at the green stains on his hands, exclaiming, "Grass has blood like people, but it's green blood." He has observed the moisture on his fingers, recalled what he knows about blood, and made a connection between the two. He has drawn a conclusion that is not exactly accurate but does use both

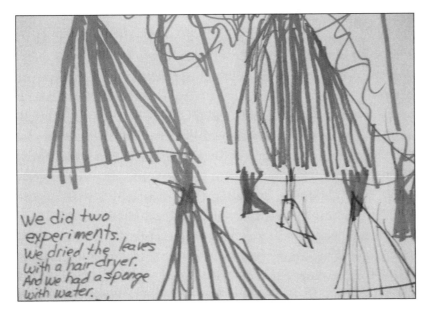
Example of a child's illustration and dictated words.

logic and creativity. Ideally, in a learning community, mistaken conclusions are seen as opportunities for deeper learning. In this example, the conversation could lead to explorations and learning about the similarities and differences between plants and people. The end result of this child's "mistake" is an unusually deep and nuanced understanding of the core concepts of biology before the child even enters kindergarten.

Making Predictions

When we make predictions we are using information, facts, or ideas to guess what will come next. Suppose a child sits at the classroom window, ignoring the teacher's repeated requests to clean up the puzzles so the class can go play outside. Exasperated, the teacher asks, "Why aren't you cleaning up?" The child replies, "Because we can't go outside. It's going to start raining soon." The child has been observing the dark clouds collecting on the horizon, and he calls upon his previous knowledge of weather to make an informed prediction about what will happen next. In this example, the teacher might use the child's prediction as a starting point for an inquiry-based project related to the weather that involves graphing the child's predictions over time.

Inquiry-Based Learning

Inquiry-based learning is a learning process that is driven by children's questions. It is not about the need to teach children predetermined concepts or facts. Using children's questions to drive the curriculum, whether by adopting the scientific process or by using other curriculum structures, results in a rich, participatory learning experience that is especially beneficial to exceptionally bright children. An inquiry-based approach naturally incorporates all three strategies of differentiation, conversation, and connection.

Fortunately, in early childhood education there is already a wide variety of inquiry-based curriculum models that benefit all children but are especially important for challenging exceptionally bright children in the area of science. The most successful inquiry-based models in early childhood include the project approach, as developed and described in many books by educators such as Lilian Katz, Sylvia Chard, and Judy Harris Helm. A similar approach that involves building projects around emerging interests is the Reggio Emilia approach, as described in books by educators such as Carolyn Edwards, Lella Gandini, George Forman, and Louise Cadwell.

Both the project approach and the Reggio Emilia approach are examples of an "emergent" curriculum process that is facilitated by teachers but led by children's interests and questions. In both approaches an emergent topic is explored over a period of time, usually by the whole class though often there are subtopics that are explored by small groups within the class. Children ask questions, make predictions, collect data, analyze their findings, and share their conclusions. Documenting learning through dictation, photographs, drawings, and other methods provides information that helps to shape the path of the project, assess children's growth, and stimulate children's reflection and meta-cognition. Children and teachers may use a variety of media to create documentation and represent what they know. Art materials, both two- and three-dimensional, and other media (for instance, dance) are used to explore what Reggio Emilia educators call "the hundred languages of children."

Steps in Developing an Emergent Project

1. Teachers observe children's play and conversations, taking note of possible topics for study. Ideally, teachers lead a consensus-building process among themselves and the children to determine the topic of focus.
2. Teachers lead activities (for example, story dictation and discussion) that reveal what children already know about the topic.
3. Children brainstorm questions and conduct research using books and primary sources (such as field trips, nature walks, and interviews).
4. Children design ways to share their findings, through drawings, photos, dictation, sculpture, and dramatization.
5. Teachers facilitate children's reflection and self-evaluation. Children review the original questions they asked about the topic and reflect on what they learned.

These inquiry-based, emergent approaches are particularly suited for exploring science topics because of the emphasis on open-ended exploration and discovery. The process is so well suited for meeting the needs of exceptionally bright young children because the group work and documentation process provide natural opportunities for teachers to differentiate for the more advanced learners in the class. Teachers can engage children in challenging conversations about what they are learning and group children in ways that maximize social learning and connection to each other in learning relationships.

The Role of the Lead Investigator

The processes described in this chapter are appropriate for all children in any preschool, pre-K, or kindergarten classroom. The beauty of these open-ended projects is that every child can participate at any level of ability or interest. But these projects are especially important for the exceptionally bright children because they allow them to take an idea and run with it. Often the exceptionally bright child will be the one to initiate a project, to ask the interesting questions, to light the fire that gets the rest of the class going.

Don't be afraid to develop a special role for a child who has exceptional interest, knowledge, or ability in a specific subject area or topic. As noted in chapter 1, one of the common characteristics of exceptionally bright children is that they often develop an intense and sustained interest in a single topic, trains or insects, for instance. When a classroom project is sparked by the special interest of one child, that child can be given the role of "lead investigator."

Creating the role of the lead investigator in a classroom project supports the Vygotskian notion, as described in chapter 5, that children thrive when they are learning in a social context. The concept that children learn from each other supports the idea that teachers should organize curriculum projects and group children according to their interests, not abilities. For example, an exceptionally bright child with a lot of knowledge and passion for the topic of dinosaurs could be encouraged to lead other children in gathering research using picture books, plastic models, and fossil replicas. There will likely be other children in the class who will become just as excited about dinosaurs as the lead investigator, even if their capacity to memorize, organize, and apply the facts is not as advanced as that of the exceptionally bright child. All the children in the research group will benefit from sharing their ideas and enthusiasm with each other.

Exploring Individual Passions

As much as we hope to find curriculum topics that will be of interest to all or most of the children in the class and develop a group consensus about what to investigate and explore, sometimes an exceptionally bright child develops a passion for a specific subject that is not shared by any of the other children. This was the case for Derek, described in chapter 5, who had an intense interest in trains. Derek's teacher was eventually able to create situations in which other children were motivated to participate in Derek's train projects, but this took some time.

If a child has a genuine passion for a science topic, whether the topic is trains or whales or bonsai gardening, and there are no other children who are also interested in that subject, it is time to help that child develop an individual project, much like a college student would develop an independent study project. The same inquiry-based structures discussed earlier in this chapter can be used with an individual child. Parents and siblings can also be recruited to assist the child in her exploration of her passion. Teachers should still look for opportunities to engage other children in the process, such as inviting the child to present the progress of her research at morning circle time.

The story dictation and dramatization techniques described in chapter 6 can also be used to present scientific information to the class in a way that engages children both as actors and as audience. If an exceptionally bright child who is fascinated with the science of extreme weather were invited to dictate a story about hurricanes, it might read something like this:

Hurricane Story

Hurricanes start over the ocean. The inside of it is warm and that makes the air spin and spin all around it. Once there was a hurricane called Katrina. It was really bad for people and flooded a lot of places.

Like fictionalized stories children dictate, scientific stories can be acted out by the children in the class. The children acting out the story could take turns being the hurricane. One child could be a hurricane that starts over the ocean. Another could be the air that spins. And another could be Katrina. The involvement of the other children in the dramatization of the story might spark their interest in hurricanes. A project that began as an independent study might become an inquiry-based group project. But even if the rest of the class never develops an interest in the topic, the process of sharing the story with the class through dramatization is an affirming experience for the child who dictated the story and developed the project.

Engineering and Technology

Looking through a catalog of children's books, you might get the impression that science is just about nature and animals. Those are the topics most commonly addressed in an early childhood curriculum. But some exceptionally bright children develop a special interest and aptitude for engineering and technology. These are important branches of science as well. A child with an intense curiosity about how things work needs opportunities to take things apart. Finding machines and appliances that can be safely deconstructed can be a challenge. Because computers, televisions, and many electronics contain chemicals and other hazardous materials, children should not be allowed to dismantle them.

Machines with very simple components, such as windup clocks or rotary telephones, can be safely taken apart, though children should still be well supervised during the process. Another option is to create a collection of pieces of machines, such as gears, springs, pipes, wire, and levers (taking care to avoid anything sharp or potentially dangerous), that children can use to make their own contraptions. Add some pieces of wood or cardboard for bases and a supply of tape and string to help hold things together and you'll be amazed at what children are able to create.

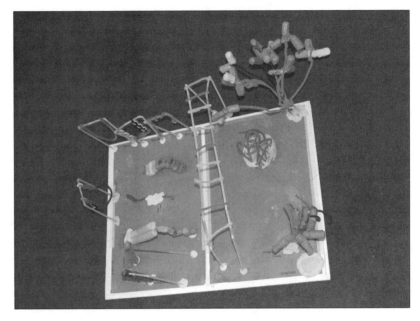

An example of a playground structure made from chenille stems and modeling clay.

Technology

Technology is both a tool for teaching science and a subject of science study. The National Science Foundation and other leading groups in science and education use the acronym STEM to refer to four subjects: science, technology, engineering, and math. STEM educators and researchers advocate for the development and expansion of education that integrates all four subjects using innovative and engaging learning experiences. For more information and resources, visit the STEM Education Resource Center at www.pbs.org /teachers/stem.

Technology can be used in an early childhood classroom to support exceptionally bright children in their explorations of science and engineering topics. Online tools and resources are available to teachers through sites such as PBS Building Big, found at www.pbs.org/wgbh/buildingbig/index.html. With support from a teacher, interactive web activities designed to teach science to older children, such as the Annenberg Foundation's Amusement Park Physics, can be played by exceptionally bright young children. The website is www.learner.org/interactives/parkphysics/index.html.

Architecture

Architecture is a multidisciplinary area of study that involves both engineering and technology, along with healthy doses of math and art. Many children enjoy playing with blocks, but children with advanced skills and interests in design and construction may benefit from learning about the field of architecture. As described in chapter 7, play with blocks and other construction materials helps children learn early geometry skills. In addition to developing math skills, young children can learn engineering concepts through experiences with building towers, digging tunnels, and constructing bridges. Children with an interest in or aptitude for architecture can be encouraged to learn more about specific buildings, such as the Eiffel Tower or the pyramids of Egypt, or to learn about famous architects, such as Frank Lloyd Wright or Mies van der Rohe. These topics can become the subject of an individual or class project. Photographs, illustrations, and blueprints can be used in the block area to guide and inspire children's constructions. Picture books like *Iggy Peck, Architect* by Andrea Beaty introduce children to the role of an architect. Online resources for teaching architecture to children include www.archkidecture.org.

Develop a Panel of Experts

Teaching exceptionally bright children can be a humbling experience, because sometimes the children's abilities, skills, and knowledge exceed our own. This can be especially true on topics related to engineering and technology. Don't be afraid to say, "I don't know," when a child asks you a question that pushes beyond your own experience and training. Use this as an opportunity to model a learning process that involves seeking expert advice. Consult with a public librarian on books and other media resources on the topics that interest the children in your class. The faculty at local colleges and universities may also be good resources for specialized information. Local experts in the field of science, engineering, and technology are likely to be pleased and flattered that you would seek them out. Don't be shy about inviting them to visit your classroom. As when any outside visitor is coming, be sure to plan and supervise the event carefully, perhaps coaching the guest ahead of time about how to present information in a developmentally appropriate fashion. An engineering professor might demonstrate a robotic arm and explain how robotic appliances are designed and constructed. Perhaps she could also bring a photo of herself as a young child and share stories of her own childhood experiences that led to a career in engineering.

Encourage Mistakes

One of the important lessons we can teach children is the value of making mistakes. Some of the most significant scientific discoveries were made by accident, such as Alexander Fleming's 1928 discovery of penicillin when he accidentally let a strange fungus grow on his culture samples. Exceptionally bright children, who may already have become accustomed to always getting the "right" answer in school, benefit from working with teachers who embrace mistakes as a sign of creative exploration. Who knows? The child making brilliant mistakes in your classroom today could one day invent a medicine or machine or process that will benefit countless people.

Classroom Strategies for Supporting Social-Emotional Development

Chapter 9

Social-Emotional Challenges

This chapter focuses not on an area of strength for exceptionally bright children but rather on an area of possible weakness: social-emotional development. Not all exceptionally bright children struggle with social-emotional issues; some have naturally warm, playful, or charismatic personalities and make friends easily. But many do have a hard time making positive social connections with others. Many children with special talents or advanced academic ability struggle, at all ages, with making and maintaining friendships. Sometimes this is because they have a hard time finding other children their age who share the same interests. Sometimes this is because they lack specific social skills that are necessary for making and maintaining friendships.

Developmentally, children between the ages of three and five are beginning to become interested in social relationships outside their own families. In a preschool classroom, making friends requires the ability to ask another child to play or being receptive to an invitation to play and the flexibility to adapt and negotiate with another child during play. Children who are exceptionally bright often struggle with initiating and sustaining play relationships with other children. Some children have a hard time reading the social cues of other children and misjudge when another child is open and willing to play.

Other children may be so absorbed in their own passions and interests that they have trouble giving up control and letting other children take the lead during play.

As discussed earlier, the development of children with advanced cognitive ability is often asynchronous; they are ahead in one developmental domain but delayed in others. Social development or physical development may be lagging behind. Delays in a young child's physical development, whether in the area of large-motor skills or small-motor skills or both, can also have an effect on social relationships. A child who struggles with coordination in running, jumping, and climbing may have a hard time literally keeping up with other children on the playground, where many social connections are forged. These children will need the nurturing support of parents, teachers, and caregivers to help them make social connections with other children.

Social-Emotional Characteristics of Exceptionally Bright Children

Some additional social-emotional characteristics of exceptionally bright children include:

Sensitivity. Heightened emotional sensitivity is a well-documented characteristic of academically gifted children in the primary and secondary grades, and the same sensitivity can certainly be observed among exceptionally bright preschool children as well. This sensitivity may be internal, meaning the child's feelings are easily hurt by any perceived slight or criticism. The sensitivity may also be external, meaning the child is especially aware of the feelings and struggles of other people.

Perfectionism. Children who are exceptionally bright are often perfectionists. Their advanced understanding and their ability to visualize their goals cause them to have very high expectations of themselves. Children with a tendency for perfectionism may work very slowly on each task, such as a drawing or a block construction, taking great care with each detail. They may also become easily frustrated, ripping up their drawings or toppling their blocks if their work doesn't meet their own high standards. Some children may not even attempt to draw or build if they are not completely confident that they will be successful.

Intense emotions. All kinds of emotions, from joy to frustration, can be especially intense among exceptionally bright children, and they may swing from one emotion to another quickly. "Excitable" and "moody" are words that are often used by parents and teachers to describe children with advanced cognitive ability. These children are also sometimes accused of "overreacting" to both good and bad experiences, because their emotional reactions can be very strong.

Introversion. Some exceptionally bright children prefer to spend much of their time alone. Sometimes this is because they lack the social skills to interact with other children, but sometimes this is because they genuinely crave solitude and the uninterrupted freedom to pursue their own interests.

Extroversion, need to control. Some exceptionally bright children are very outgoing. They may be leaders during dramatic play or during active games on the playground. Along with the ability to lead others, exceptionally bright children may also be excessively controlling of other children and have a hard time letting others have a say.

Adult focus. Many exceptionally bright young children seek out the company of adults for conversation. Often this is because the other children their own age do not share the same interests, level of understanding, or sophistication of language.

Sophisticated sense of humor. Some exceptionally bright children possess a sense of humor that is well beyond their years. For example, while other preschool children enjoy "potty talk" and slapstick humor, an exceptionally bright young child may enjoy puns and word play. In rare cases, an especially advanced child might begin to understand or even use sarcasm, a characteristic usually not seen until much later in childhood.

Facilitating Friendships

One of the most important roles of an early childhood teacher is facilitating friendships between children. This is true for all the children but may be especially valuable for exceptionally bright children who have trouble making connections with their peers. The following suggestions for facilitating friendships may be helpful for any socially reluctant child, but they may be especially helpful for children on the autism spectrum or children with Asperger's syndrome. As discussed in chapter 1, children with autism have

Children making friends over a shared interest in bees.

difficulty communicating with other children, and children with Asperger's syndrome are often socially awkward. If a child in your classroom is diagnosed with one of these conditions, seek out suggestions and ideas from the child's parents. It is likely that the child's physician and therapists have developed specific routines and strategies for supporting the child's social interactions. Here are a few strategies for successfully facilitating friendships between exceptionally bright young children and their typically developing peers and one strategy that includes older children.

Create Pairs

Any young child who struggles to make friends will benefit when the teacher facilitates the creation of pairs and small groups for play and activities. Often just a suggestion (*Why don't you play with James?*) will not be enough. Assign children to work together on short activities, such as setting napkins out on the snack table (*James and Maggie, it's your turn to set the table for snack*). Give the exceptionally bright child a task that highlights her talent (*Maggie, please count the napkins to make sure we have enough*) and give the other children tasks too, so everyone has something important to do (*James, please put a cracker basket on each table*). Perhaps, as in this example, the children who have collaborated together could also be invited to sit together during snack and take turns describing for the group how they worked together to accomplish their goal.

Find Common Ground

Exceptionally bright children sometimes feel like other children their own age don't share their interests and passions. It may be true that the child has one area of intense interest, such as submarines or centaurs, that is not equally shared by other children, but the teacher can help the children find other areas of common ground. Sometimes it is helpful to create a list of a child's potential interests outside the one topic of intense passion. Interview the exceptionally bright child and ask about her preferences for play, stories, books, food, playground equipment, and so on, and create a written list. Keep the list handy in the classroom and whenever the child is struggling to find a friend or make a connection, use the list to facilitate conversations and play between children. Note: As much as educators like to discourage screen time for young children, sometimes TV shows, movies, and computer games are good sources of conversation starters and play prompts. If a group of children frequently pretend to be Star Wars characters on the playground, the exceptionally bright child who has trouble making friends could be encouraged to learn more about one of the characters, by talking to the children or by watching the movies, so he could more actively participate in the pretend play.

Teach Children How to Join Play

Children who struggle with making friends often need adults to give them very specific instructions and ideas for how to go about making connections with other children. We need to teach them how to join other children in play. If a child wants to join children who are engaged in pretend play, she may need instructions from the teacher for how to choose a role that will fit into the pretend scenario. The teacher may need to be explicit and say, for example, "The children are pretending to be mice. What kind of mouse do you want to be? What would one mouse say to another mouse?"

Children who are accustomed to being solely focused on their own thoughts and interests may also benefit from being reminded to say friendly and kind things to their friends to show their appreciation (*I like what you made*; or *It's fun to play with you*).

Mixed-Age Groups

While exceptionally bright children certainly benefit from learning to make friends with their peers, it can be helpful to explore opportunities for these children to interact with and have conversations with older children as well. If your preschool classroom is part of a larger program that also serves school-age children, perhaps some special opportunities could be created for mixed-age activities. One idea is to invite a school-age child who enjoys playing strategy games, such as chess, to visit the preschool classroom and teach an exceptionally bright preschool child how to play the game.

Use Your Words

For any emotional struggles experienced by exceptionally bright children, the best strategy is helping children name and express their feelings. When children are frustrated or upset, try to reflect and describe what you see (*I noticed you threw your picture in the garbage. You seem unhappy*). Instead of glossing over a child's concern with reassurances (*Your drawings are great!*), ask open-ended questions that might help the child identify the source of frustration (*How do you want your drawing to look?*).

For exceptionally bright children, finding the right words to express the complexity of their emotions may be especially challenging. A child may feel a mix of contradictory emotions. When another child refuses to play with her, she may feel both angry and relieved. Ask the child questions and offer words that might describe her feelings, but use language that is open to other possibilities (*Janie, I noticed that Bianca didn't want to play with you. Did that make you mad? Are you having lots of different feelings about it?*).

As always, take time to really listen to children's responses before jumping in with more questions or suggestions. Over time, modeling language that describes feelings will help children begin to use their own words to both express their emotions and create their own strategies and plans for overcoming frustration or disappointment.

On Being Different

During the preschool years, as children begin to have more experiences outside their own families, peer relations become more and more important. Developmentally, this is the time when children are moving from parallel play to cooperative play. Even young children, as early as age three or four, are aware of what it means to fit in and be part of a social group. The little girl who refuses to wear pants because "all the girls wear dresses" is expressing her emerging sense of identity and her desire to fit into a larger group. A child may feel anxiety if she senses that she is different from other children in some way. For example, a child with bright red curly hair may sometimes enjoy the extra attention she receives about her hair, but there will certainly be times when she will feel self-conscious about it and even seek to hide her hair under a hat to avoid both negative and positive attention. Being exceptionally bright is not a characteristic as visible as bright red hair, but any kind of difference may cause children both pleasure and anxiety.

A child who is exceptionally bright may sense that she is different from other children in some way, but she may not yet be able to articulate what that difference is. Even the adults in the child's life, her parents, teachers, and caregivers, may not yet be clear about the child's strengths and talents, particularly if no formal evaluation or screening has been done. This uncertainty creates the potential for heightened anxiety, for both the child and her parents, because there is only a cloudy, vague sense that the child is somehow different from her peers.

For children who are especially bright and possess truly exceptional intellectual abilities, there may also be a growing sense that in addition to being different or smarter than their peers, they are different from the adults as well. Again, even the brightest young child may not be able to express this perception in words, but it is possible for a child to sense that he has understanding and abilities beyond those of some of the adults in his life. Imagine the intense mix of pleasure and fear that might cause a child. He may sense or know he is smarter than some of his teachers, yet he depends on them to care for him, protect him, and keep him safe. As a result, some exceptionally bright children may try to hide their strengths and abilities. A child may pretend he doesn't know how to read, may refuse to participate in class discussions, or may deliberately give the wrong answer to teachers' questions.

Cultural Influences

In addition to the desire to fit in, a child may also be struggling with unspoken issues related to culture and gender. For example, some cultures place a lot of value on group identity over and above individual achievement. Children coming from families with this value system may feel extra pressure to fit in and not call attention to themselves. In contrast, some families and cultures value academic achievement highly and parents may actively seek to have their children singled out as academically talented. The issue of gender can be especially complex with regard to academic achievement. There is extensive research to confirm that many cultures—including mainstream culture in the United States—through traditions, the media, and other methods, communicate that it is better for girls and women to be pretty and nice than to be smart and powerful. As one example, slogans on school-age girls' T-shirts sold in popular department stores in the fall of 2011 included "Allergic to Algebra" and "I'm too pretty to do homework so my brother has to do it for me" (Ng 2011). Girls with special interests and talents in the areas of math and science are especially vulnerable to this kind of pressure. Exceptionally bright young girls may need extra encouragement and support so they are prepared to counteract the messages that much of the media and society at large send them.

Parents, as well as educators, may unintentionally reinforce these cultural messages about gender in the ways they respond to children; for example, complimenting a girl for her pretty skirt or her quiet compliance or complimenting a boy for how fast he can run or for the tough questions he asks during circle time. Adults who work with young children must be intentional about how we praise and encourage children in order to ensure that girls are also supported in their efforts to be strong athletes and critical thinkers.

The Teacher's Role

Teachers can support exceptionally bright young children in their development of identities that go against the grain of popular culture. We can provide encouragement, set high expectations for all children, and serve as or provide positive role models. It is also important that all young children, regardless of cognitive ability, receive consistent, nurturing care. In early childhood programs all children benefit when we set clear limits and follow predictable schedules and routines. Throughout this book you have been encouraged to adapt your curriculum and instructional practices to accommodate the individual differences among the children, but in terms of classroom management and supervision, the key is consistency and predictability. All children, including exceptionally bright children, need the security of clear limits. They need to know that an adult is in charge and will keep them safe.

Imaginary Friends

Exceptionally bright young children tend to have vivid imaginations. It is not unusual for a child with a vivid imagination to create an imaginary friend. Sometimes the friend is another child, sometimes it is an animal, sometimes it is a character based on a story or television show, and sometimes it is wholly original, such as the four-year-old boy who saves a spot at the snack table for his imaginary friend, Dwij, a baby robot. Pretending that they have special friends that only they can see can be very satisfying for young children. It is a great opportunity to be in control and practice the feelings and rituals of friendship. Sometimes parents and teachers are concerned when children create imaginary friends, especially if the children refuse to acknowledge that the friends are imaginary. Keep in mind that imaginary friends are especially common among creative, bright children who spend a fair amount of time in solitary play. Let the child take the lead: If a child is open and talkative about having an imaginary friend, don't be afraid to play along and share in the child's enjoyment. However, if you notice that the child is more comfortable keeping his imaginary friend a quiet secret, respect the child's privacy by not calling attention to the imaginary friendship.

Helping the World

As mentioned earlier, some exceptionally bright children also have an exceptional awareness of the emotions and struggles of the people around them. They may even have a growing awareness of current events and social issues in the larger world, gleaned from listening to adult conversations or news stories. For some of these children this kind of awareness about difficult issues, such as pollution, global warming, or homelessness, can bring a heightened level of anxiety. An age-appropriate introduction to social action can be a helpful antidote to this anxiety. For these children, gently introducing them to some form of social action or community service will give them opportunities to express and build on their strong empathy and concern for others.

Listen to and observe children, talk with parents, and look for a common theme or issue that might emerge that best demonstrates the child's focus in her concerns about people and the world. For very young children, sometimes their first act of community service is related to animals, for instance, collecting blankets for a local animal shelter. Once you (and the child's family) have identified an area of concern and some specific action that the child wants to get involved in, other children can be invited to join the cause. A list of suggested resources for helping children become involved in social action or community service is provided in appendix A. These kinds of service activities are also great ways to help the exceptionally bright child develop leadership skills and make friends.

Working with Parents and Families of Exceptionally Bright Children

What Are Parents Concerned About?

As early childhood professionals we are in the position of being among the first educators parents encounter in their children's lives. We may be the first ones parents come to when they begin wondering if their child is unusually bright or perhaps academically gifted. While the parents may be feeling pride and excitement in discovering their children's unusual abilities and strengths, they often simultaneously have deep concerns about their children's future. Here are some of the concerns parents of exceptionally bright children may be experiencing and my thoughts on how to address them.

Academic Challenge

Many parents of exceptionally bright young children are beginning to wonder whether a traditional school setting can meet the needs of their child. For these parents, listening to their concerns is always the most valuable first step. Answer their questions about what you are seeing in the classroom and provide them with specific examples. If you are meeting at a formal parent-teacher conference, bring samples of the child's artwork, dictation or writing, photos of projects, and any other documentation you may have available that demonstrates the child's experience in your classroom.

Parents of exceptionally bright children may be worried that their child won't be challenged in your classroom. They may say this to you directly, or they may imply it in their expressions of concern about their child's future. Use the strategies in this book to explain how you are differentiating the curriculum, engaging their child in challenging conversations, and connecting their child with other children in learning relationships. Parents are not likely to have training and experience in developmentally appropriate practice, so take time to explain it to them and show them examples of the ways that cognitive challenges for very young children are likely to involve hands-on projects and creative conversations, rather than worksheets and encyclopedias. As the school year progresses, continue to provide parents with specific examples of the activities and strategies you are using to differentiate the curriculum and the classroom to meet their child's needs.

Assessment

If parents ask for more information than you can provide or seem stuck on what to do next, a suggestion for screening or evaluation may be appropriate. Information about assessment can be found in chapter 2. Parents can also be referred to online resources, such as the website for the National Association for Gifted Children, listed in appendix B. A developmental evaluation may provide helpful information, especially if a child seems to have significantly asynchronous development—advanced in one area but delayed in another. Parents may also need to hear your reminders that children grow and develop very rapidly in the early years and that testing in early childhood is not a sure predictor of future development or achievement.

Anxiety and Perfectionism

Parents of children who are exceptionally bright may be concerned when their child seems anxious or displays perfectionism. Again, reassure parents that these characteristics are often seen in exceptionally bright children and support the family in their efforts to provide balance and set limits. Parents may appreciate your suggestions for how to talk with their child, for example, by asking open-ended questions that draw out the child's feelings and making statements that acknowledge and reflect the child's feelings. Encourage families to create predictable household routines, including a general schedule and reasonable time limits on activities that their child may tend to overdo. Young children may benefit from being told directly, "It's okay to make mistakes. We learn more from our mistakes than from our successes."

Remind parents that children benefit from praise that emphasizes their effort, not just their success in finding the "right" answer. If a parent reports that her child gets easily frustrated playing with Lego blocks because he's not able to re-create the elaborate spaceship featured on the cover of the toy catalog, encourage the parent to draw the child's attention to the unique and innovative features the child has been able to build into his structure, such as a shuttle dock or a landing pod.

Friendships

When an exceptionally bright child is a loner, either because she has trouble making friends or because she prefers to play by herself, it is often the parents who

Tracing puddles is something family members can do together to support their child's curiosity about what happens to water when it evaporates.

are more concerned than the child. One of the main reasons families enroll their children in preschool and pre-K programs is for socialization. If parents don't see their children forming friendships and playing with other children, it is understandable that they would feel concerned. Be sure to involve parents in your plans to facilitate friendships between their child and other children. Seek their advice and suggestions and keep them closely informed of their child's progress. Share with parents some of the strategies described in the previous chapters, for instance, teaching children the words to say when they want to play with someone else. Again, many of the resources for parents in appendix B might be useful to families in their efforts to support their child's social skills.

Parent-Child Relationships

Sometimes parents of exceptionally bright young children feel anxious or frustrated about their own interactions with their children. Parents of a moody, intense child may need advice about how to handle the child's outbursts and temper tantrums. Usually the same advice you would give any family about discipline issues is going to apply to parents of exceptionally bright children as well. The only difference is that parents might need extra reassurance that even though their child has some exceptional cognitive talents, he is still very young emotionally. Parents of a child with advanced verbal skills may actually feel intimidated by their child and his ability to argue and debate with them. Again, encourage parents to set clear, reasonable limits for behavior and let them know it's okay to end an argument or conversation if they feel the child is pushing them too hard. The conversation can be revisited after everyone has had time to calm down and think clearly.

The Role of Family Culture

Every time we seek to understand and communicate with families, which is, I hope, every single day we work with children, the best place to start is with the assumption that partnering with parents and families will always benefit children. One of the most important strategies for connecting with families is an openness and awareness of the role culture plays in every family. Janet Gonzalez-Mena and Dora Pulido-Tobiassen (1999) maintain that everything a family does is influenced by that family's culture. So it stands to reason that how a family raises an exceptionally bright child, including how the parents respond to the child's special gifts, is also going to be influenced by culture:

> Almost every aspect of child-rearing—including feeding, diapering, and toilet training—is influenced by cultural beliefs and values. How we talk to young children, touch them, bathe them, dress them, and see to their napping needs are all cultural behaviors. Over time, children learn who they are and what to do through these experiences—absorbing a sense of their routines, traditions, languages, cultures, and national or racial identities. There are many equally valid ways to raise healthy children who thrive in the world. Professional knowledge and experience are important, but we must never forget how much we can learn from the families we work with.

It can be hard for teachers to resist judging parents for the choices they make for their children. When working with exceptionally bright young children, we might wonder if a parent is doing too much or too little to nurture a child's advanced cognitive abilities. Maybe you see parents enroll their child in a weekend tutoring program and you feel that it will put too much pressure on the child to learn academic skills too soon. Or perhaps you see parents who seem to be ignoring their child's talents and you want them to take more notice of the unique gifts the child has to offer.

The best way to resist the urge to judge families is to get to know them, to observe, to listen, to ask questions, and to welcome them into your classroom. When you become aware that a family's values and practices are different from your own or different from what you might recommend as an early childhood professional, take some time to reflect before you take any action to express your ideas to the family. Talk with another early childhood professional, perhaps your supervisor or a trusted colleague, and see if you can sort through what role your own culture and beliefs are playing in the conclusions you have drawn about this family. When in doubt, wait. Observe and listen as you continue to get to know the family better.

In addition to cultural differences, linguistic differences sometimes make it more difficult for you to communicate with a family and create a strong partnership with them. Seek out appropriate translation and interpretation services as needed.

How to Offer Support

In summary, the best strategies for teachers to support parents and families of children who are exceptionally bright include these:

Listening. Find the right time and place to listen to parents' concerns and questions. Don't jump in right away with suggestions and resources. Try to get to the heart of what parents most fear and most hope for their children. Keep in mind that many parents of exceptionally bright children were once exceptionally bright children themselves. Their parenting may be influenced by their own positive and negative experiences as children.

Asking what they need. Don't assume that parents are looking for something specific, such as a referral for screening and evaluation services. Ask parents what they need and how you can help. Then listen to their answers.

Helping parents recognize their child's cues. Sometimes when parents are struggling to understand or communicate with their child, they just need a gentle reminder to slow down and watch or listen, in order to recognize their child's cues and needs. Model this for parents in the ways you interact with children in the classroom and in the ways you interact with their child when the family is together. Informal family events like picnics and potluck dinners are great times to have these kinds of interactions.

Offering reassurance and affirmation. Parents of exceptionally bright children are usually looking for two seemingly contradictory things: they want reassurance that their child is perfectly normal, and they want recognition that their child is special. You can certainly give them both of these things. Children who are exceptionally bright are perfectly "normal" children. They need their parents' love and acceptance, the friendship and companionship of other children, and the guidance and support of their teachers and other adults in their lives. They need all these things just as deeply as any other child. They are also special. They have the gift of being able to see and understand the world in a way that is different from that of many other children. Your job is to help parents keep these two realities in harmonious balance as you work with them to lay a foundation for a lifetime of joyous learning.

Recommended Resources for Teachers

Early Literacy Online Resources

The Horn Book

www.hbook.com

The Horn Book magazine is considered an essential guide to children's and young adult literature. The magazine's website includes reviews and recommendations for young readers (click on "Choosing Books").

Kidsreads

www.kidsreads.com

Kidsreads is part of the online Book Report Network, a family of book-related sites that offer book reviews, author profiles, feature articles, and contests. This is a commercial site, but the quality of both the books they feature and the online content is very good.

Reading Lists for Your Gifted Child

www.hoagiesgifted.org/reading_lists.htm

This collection of links to reading lists focused on academically gifted children is part of Hoagies' Gifted Education Page, a popular hub of gifted education information for both parents and professionals.

Math Resources

Math-Friendly Authors

Mistumasa Anno: Author of intricately illustrated storybooks that demonstrate a wide range of mathematical concepts, from simple to complex, including

Anno's Counting Book
Anno's Counting House
The Anno's Mysterious Multiplying Jar

Anno has also written several books of math games for children, including

Anno's Math Games
Anno's Math Games 2

Tana Hoban: Author of picture books featuring vivid photographs that teach simple geometry concepts, such as

Shapes, Shapes, Shapes
Is It Larger? Is It Smaller?
Over, Under and Through
So Many Circles, So Many Squares

Stuart J. Murphy: Author of MathStart books, a series of illustrated storybooks created to introduce specific math concepts, such as

Double the Ducks
More or Less
Give Me Half!
Divide and Ride

Math-Friendly Picture Books

Spaghetti and Meatballs for All by Marilyn Burns
One Grain of Rice: A Mathematical Folktale by Demi
Two of Everything by Lily Toy Hong
The Doorbell Rang by Pat Hutchins
Actual Size by Steve Jenkins
One Monkey Too Many by Jackie French Koller
Measuring Penny by Loreen Leedy
How Big Is a Foot? by Rolf Myller

Ducks Disappearing by Phyllis Reynolds Naylor
Math Curse by Jon Scieszka
Too Many Pumpkins by Linda White
Weighing the Elephants by Ting-xing Ye

Math Online Resources

Ask Dr. Math

http://mathforum.org/dr.math

The Math Forum is hosted by Drexel University and features "Ask Dr. Math," a question-and-answer service for math students and their teachers. A searchable archive is available by level and topic.

Early Mathematics Education Project

http://earlymath.erikson.edu

The goal of the Early Mathematics Education Project of the Erikson Institute is to provide to early childhood professionals the professional development, research, and resources that support the solid introduction of early math concepts to young children. The project website offers valuable information, recommended links, and resources.

Khan Academy

www.khanacademy.org

The Khan Academy is a not-for-profit organization offering "free world-class education for anyone anywhere." Online lessons in math and science are helpful resources for teachers who want to brush up on their knowledge and skills or prepare advanced content for exceptionally bright students.

Mathcats

http://mathcats.com

Mathcats is an award-winning site offering online games and activities for children of all ages. Recommended by the National Council of Teachers of Mathematics, the site is created and operated by math teacher Wendy Petti.

National Council of Teachers of Mathematics

www.nctm.org

The website of the NCTM offers lessons and resources for teachers as well as access to national standards and Curriculum Focal Points, "the most important math topics for lasting learning at each grade level Pre-K–8."

NCTM Resources for Teaching Math
http://illuminations.nctm.org
Illuminations is a resource page developed by the National Council of Teachers of Mathematics to offer activities, lessons, standards, and web links for pre-K through grade 12.

PBS Teacher Math Resources
www.pbs.org/teachers/classroom/prek/math/resources
PBS Teachers is an extensive website offering classroom resources. Many, but not all, of the resources are related to PBS television programming. The site allows visitors to search for pre-K-specific resources in the area of math.

S.O.S. Mathematics
www.sosmath.com
S.O.S. Mathematics is intended for high school and adult learners who are seeking easy-to-read and accessible information about math topics. This is a good site for adults who want help reviewing basic math concepts.

Recommended Math Books for Teachers

The Young Child and Mathematics by Juanita V. Copely
Spotlight on Young Children and Math, edited by Derry Koralek

Recommended Math-Related Mobile Applications

Musical Me! by Duck Duck Moose
http://duckduckmoosedesign.com/educational-iphone-itouch-apps-for-kids/musical-me
Animal characters create note patterns and rhythms.

Slice It! by Com2uS Inc.
http://itunes.apple.com/us/app/slice-it!/id388116298?mt=8
Divide various shapes into equal size pieces.

Science Online Resources

B4UBuild Stuff for Kids
www.b4ubuild.com/kids/kidlinks.html
This is a commercial site affiliated with residential construction services that offers links to a variety of online resources for engineering and architecture activities and books for children.

Kids.gov Life Science Resources
www.kids.gov/k_5/k_5_science_life.shtml
Kids.gov is the official portal to U.S. government information and services on the web geared to the learning levels and interests of children. The Life Science section offers information about plants, animals, and living things, as well as information about inventors and scientists, science fair projects, and careers in science.

Kidshealth.org
http://kidshealth.org/kid
The KidsHealth site is part of the Nemours Foundation's Center for Children's Health Media and offers information and resources about health and biology topics geared to kids, teens, and parents.

Museum of Science and Industry
www.msichicago.org/education/educator-resources/classroom-activities
The Museum of Science and Industry in Chicago offers a searchable database of activity and lesson plans for preschool to adults on a wide range of science topics.

National Science Center
www.nscdiscovery.org
The National Science Center is a nonprofit organization in partnership with the United States Army with a mission to increase students' interest in science and math. The website offers resources for educators as well as links and games for children.

National Science Teachers Association
www.nsta.org/elementaryschool/?lid=hp
The NSTA is a membership organization providing resources and advocacy for science educators. The Elementary Science web page offers curriculum articles and lesson plans that would also be relevant for advanced preschoolers.

North American Reggio Emilia Alliance
www.reggioalliance.org
The North American Reggio Emilia Alliance (NAREA) is a network of educators and parents inspired by the philosophies and experiences of the 0–6 education project of Reggio Emilia, Italy. The NAREA website offers information about the history and philosophy of Reggio Emilia as well as professional development opportunities for educators.

PBS Kids ZOOM Science
http://pbskids.org/zoom/activities/sci
Based on the *ZOOM* show on PBS, the "ZOOM Sci" web pages offer fun science activities created and tested by kids. Activities categories are Chemistry, Engineering, The Five Senses, Forces & Energy, Life Science, Patterns, Sound, Structures, and Water.

The Project Approach
www.projectapproach.org
This site is managed by educator and author Sylvia Chard and offers a broad range of information about the Project Approach, including an overview of the theoretical framework, explanations for how to develop project work, and examples of projects conducted in classrooms worldwide.

Research Skills for Kids
http://kidsspace.torontopubliclibrary.ca/research.html
This online research guide from the Toronto Public Library breaks down the research process into four simple steps. Access to some of the links requires a TPL library card, but the general information the site offers can be helpful to teachers and parents.

Science NetLinks
www.sciencenetlinks.com
Science NetLinks is a project of the American Association for the Advancement of Science. The site offers teaching tools, interactive games, podcasts, and hands-on activities for teachers, students, and parents.

U.S. Fish and Wildlife Service: Let's Go Outside!
www.fws.gov/letsgooutside/kids.html
This online resource for kids, families, and educators includes a free searchable digital library of images and videos of animals, plants, and fish. The website also offers helpful information for educators, such as suggestions for creating schoolyard habitats and planning outdoor trips.

Social Action/Community Service Online Resources

Community Service Ideas
www.kidactivities.net/post/Community-Service-Ideas-for-Kids.aspx
Kidsactivities.net is a network of online resources for child care providers. This page offers a list of community service projects for children of all ages.

Do Something
www.dosomething.org
Do Something is a nonprofit organization providing information, grants, and awards for youth volunteers. The focus is on teenagers, but much of the information is relevant for volunteers of all ages who want to make a difference in their community.

A Family's Guide to Getting Involved
http://kidshealth.org/parent/positive/family/volunteer.html
This page, which is part of the Nemour Foundation's Center for Children's Health Media's KidsHealth site, offers an article for parents about the benefits of community service and ideas for getting involved.

Help the Homeless
www.hud.gov/kids/hthsplsh.html
This is a kid-friendly site operated by the U.S. Department of Housing and Urban Development that answers questions such as "Who are the homeless?" and "What can kids do to help?"

Kids Helping Animals
www.paws.org/e-news-kids.html
This site is operated by PAWS, an organization based in Washington State that provides rehabilitation, medical care, shelter, and adoption services for both wild and domesticated animals. *Kids Helping Animals* is a downloadable newsletter for children with articles about kids who make a difference in the lives of homeless, ill, or injured animals.

National Service-Learning Clearinghouse
www.servicelearning.org
The NSLC supports service-learning for students from kindergarten through higher education. The website offers information and resources to support service-learning programs, practitioners, and researchers.

Resources for Parents and Families

Recommended Books

How to Get Your Child to Love Reading by Esmé Raji Codell

Some of My Best Friends Are Books: Guiding Gifted Readers from Preschool to High School by Judith Wynn Halsted

Early Gifts: Recognizing and Nurturing Children's Talents edited by Paula Olszewski-Kubilius, Lisa Limburg-Weber, and Steven Pfeiffer

Recommended Organizations and Online Resources

Hoagies' Gifted Education Page for Parents
www.hoagiesgifted.org/parents.htm
Hoagies' "All Things Gifted" is an award-winning website developed by the parent of a gifted child who wanted to share her research and experience with others. Articles and links offer information and ideas to educators, parents, and children.

NAEYC For Families
http://families.naeyc.org
The NAEYC For Families site provides families with information on finding quality child care, articles by well-known pediatricians and child development experts about how children learn, and creative learning ideas to try at home. In addition, the site contains a searchable database to help families locate centers and schools accredited by NAEYC for their infants, toddlers, and preschoolers.

NAGC Welcome Parents!
www.nagc.org/welcomeparents.aspx
The National Association for Gifted Children is a membership group focused on advocacy and professional development. NAGC offers a web page for parents with links to information and resources, such as the article "The ABCs of Gifted."

References

American Institute of Physics. 2004. "A. Einstein: Image and Impact: Formative Years I." Last modified November. www.aip.org/history/einstein/early1.htm.

Anderson, Lorin W., and David R. Krathwohl, eds. 2001. *A Taxonomy for Learning, Teaching, and Assessing: A Revision of Bloom's Taxonomy of Educational Objectives.* New York: Longman.

Autism Society. 2012. "About Autism." Accessed October 28. www.autism-society.org/about-autism.

Bennett-Armistead, V. Susan, Nell K. Duke, and Annie M. Moses. 2005. *Literacy and the Youngest Learner: Best Practices for Educators of Children from Birth to 5.* New York: Scholastic.

Bloom, Benjamin S. 1974. *Taxonomy of Educational Objectives: The Classification of Educational Goals.* New York: David McKay.

Centers for Disease Control and Prevention. 2012. "Autism Spectrum Disorders: Research." Last modified June 19. www.cdc.gov/ncbddd/autism/research.html.

Frances A. Karnes Center for Gifted Studies. n.d. *Reaching Potential: Recognizing, Understanding, and Serving Gifted Preschoolers.* Hattiesburg: University of Southern Mississippi.

Gardner, Howard. 1999. *Intelligence Reframed: Multiple Intelligences for the 21st Century*. New York: Basic Books.

———. 2006. *Multiple Intelligences: New Horizons*. New York: Basic Books.

Gaustad, Joan. 1997. "Building Support for Multiage Education." *ERIC Digest* 114. Retrieved from ERIC.ed.gov, ED409604.

Gonzalez-Mena, Janet, and Dora Pulido-Tobiassen. 1999. "Teaching 'Diversity': A Place to Begin." Scholastic.com. *Early Childhood Today* (November). www.scholastic.com/teachers/article/teaching-quotdiversityquot-place-begin.

Hoffman, Jo. 2002. "Flexible Grouping Strategies in the Multiage Classroom." *Theory into Practice* 41 (1): 47–52.

Katz, Lilian G. 1995. "The Benefits of Mixed-Age Grouping." *ERIC Digest*. Retrieved from ERIC.ed.gov, ED382411.

Kohn, Alfie. 2012. "Criticizing (Common Criticisms of) Praise." *Huffington Post Education*. Published February 3. www.huffingtonpost.com/alfie-kohn/criticizing-common-critic_b_1252344.html.

Mueller, Claudia M., and Carol S. Dweck. 1998. "Praise for Intelligence Can Undermine Children's Motivation and Performance." *Journal of Personality and Social Psychology* 75 (1): 33–52.

National Council of Teachers of Mathematics. 2012. *Executive Summary: Principles and Standards for School Mathematics*. Accessed February 17. www.nctm.org/uploadedFiles/Math_Standards/12752_exec_pssm.pdf.

Ng, Christina. 2011. "Forever 21's 'Allergic to Algebra' Shirt Draws Criticism." *Nation ABCNews Blog*. Last modified September 12. http://abcnews.go.com/blogs/headlines/2011/09/forever-21s-allergic-to-algebra-shirt-draws-criticism.

Olszewski-Kubilius, Paula, Lisa Limburg-Weber, and Steven Pfeiffer, eds. 2003. *Early Gifts: Recognizing and Nurturing Children's Talents*. Waco, TX: Prufrock Press.

Pennsylvania Department of Education and Department of Public Welfare. 2009. *Pre-Kindergarten: Pennsylvania Learning Standards for Early Childhood*, 2nd ed. Harrisburg: Pennsylvania Department of Education and Department of Public Welfare.

Pletan, Michael D., Nancy M. Robinson, Virginia W. Berninger, and Robert D. Abbott. 1995. "Parents' Observations of Math-Precocious Preschoolers." *Journal for the Education of the Gifted* 19 (1): 30–44.

Tishman, Shari, and David Perkins. 1997. "The Language of Thinking," *Phi Delta Kappan* 78 (5): 368–75.

Trelease, Jim. 1995. *The Read-Aloud Handbook*. 3rd ed. New York: Penguin Books.

Videatives. 2006. *Jed Draws His Bicycle*. CD. Amherst, MA: Videatives.

Vygotsky, Lev. 1978. *Mind in Society: The Development of Higher Psychological Processes*. Translated by Michael Cole. Cambridge, MA: Harvard University Press.

Wadsworth, Reba M. 2008. "Using Read Alouds in Today's Classrooms." National Association of Elementary School Principals. *Leadership Compass* 5 (3). www.naesp.org/resources/2/Leadership_Compass/2008/LC2008v5n3a4.pdf.

Washington State OSPI (Office of Superintendent of Public Instruction). 2008. *A Guide to Assessment in Early Childhood: Infancy to Age Eight*. Olympia: Washington State OSPI. www.k12.wa.us/EarlyLearning/pubdocs/assessment_print.pdf.

Index

characteristics and behaviors of, 1–2, 7–9, 18–19, 110–11
excelling in one curriculum area, 9–10
as lead investigators, 103
social-emotional development, 19, 109–11
supporting and meeting needs of, 3, 6, 116
terminology and labels, 14–15
twice-exceptional children, 12–14
extroversion, 111

F

families
cultural differences, 122
as information sources, 20–22, 25
resources for, 133–34
supporting, 123–24
Family's Guide to Getting Involved (website), 131
feedback for children, 55–58, 121
"five finger rule" for reading level, 74
Fleming, Alexander, 107
flexible grouping, 34, 65–66
Flotsam (Wiesner), 75
Forman, George, 24
Fox, Mem, 77
Frances A. Karnes Center for Gifted Studies, University of Southern Mississippi, 18
Fred Rogers Center (FRC), 95
friendships
facilitating, 111–13
imaginary friends, 116
parent concerns about, 121
funny books, 76

G

games, for math differentiation, 89
Gardner, Howard, 15
gender differences in science and math abilities, 95, 115
geometry, 87, 89–91
gifted children
terminology and labels for, 14–15
See also exceptionally bright children

Go, Dog. Go! (Eastman), 10
goals, setting, 57–58
Gonzalez-Mena, Janet, 122
graphic novels, 76
grouping children
ability grouping, 66
benefits of, 65
facilitating friendships, 112–13
flexible grouping, 34
mixed-age groups, 65–66, 113

H

Harvard University, Project Zero, 52
Help the Homeless (website), 131
higher-order thinking skills
creative thinking, 33, 41–42, 46
critical thinking, 33, 41–42, 45
increasing complexity, 31–33, 49–50
See also challenging activities for children
Hoagies' Gifted Education page, 125, 133
Hoban, Tana, 94, 126
Holm, Jennifer and Matthew, 76
Horn Book, The (magazine), 125
humor, sense of, 76, 111
Hunger Games, The (Collins), 75
hypothesis testing, 98–101

I

identifying exceptionally bright children. *See* assessment
Iggy Peck, Architect (Beaty), 106
imaginary friends, 116
imagination. *See* creative thinking; play
inquiry-based learning, 30–31, 102–3
instruction. *See* teaching practices
intelligence
evaluation tools, 22–23
multiple intelligences, 15–16
interests of children
exploring science, 104
facilitating friendships through, 112–13
interpersonal intelligence, 15
intrapersonal intelligence, 16
introversion, 111

measuring potential of bright children. *See* assessment

Meisels, Sam, 23

memory, of exceptionally bright children, 8–9

Mercy Watson book series (DiCamillo), 77

metacognition
    modeling, 52
    overview, 42–43
    promoting with questions, 48, 50–53

mistakes, value of, 107, 121

MKOs. *See* more knowledgeable others (MKOs)

mobile applications
    Bubble Harp, 94
    math-related, 128

more knowledgeable others (MKOs), 61–62

multiple intelligences, 15–16

Murphy, Stuart J., 94, 126

Museum of Science and Industry, 129

musical intelligence, 15

N

National Association for Gifted Children (NAGC), 120, 134

National Association for the Education of Young Children (NAEYC), 95, 134

National Council of Teachers of Mathematics, 86, 127–28

National Science Center, 129

National Science Foundation, STEM subjects, 105

National Science Teachers Association, 130

National Service-Learning Clearinghouse, 132

naturalist intelligence, 16

natural readers, 72

nonfiction books, 75–76

normed assessments, 22–23

North American Reggio Emilia Alliance, 130

number and operations, foundational skills, 86

O

observation, as assessment tool, 19–20, 25

open-ended questions, 47–49

Osborne, Mary Pope, 76

Owly book series (Runton), 76

P

pace, adapting for activities, 34–35

parents
    concerns of, 119–22
    explaining asynchronous development to, 23
    observations of math-precocious preschoolers, 84–85
    resources for, 133–34
    supporting, 123–24
    See also families

Park, Barbara, 76

PBS Building Big (website), 106

PBS Kids ZOOM Science, 130

PBS Teacher Math Resources, 128

perfectionism, 110, 120–21

Perkins, David, 52

pets, unit on
    curriculum, differentiating, 29–33
    learning environment, differentiating, 36–39
    teaching strategies, differentiating, 33–35
    See also animals

Piaget, 60

picture books
    math-friendly, 94, 126–27
    read-aloud books, 81
    selecting, 75

Picture Window Books, 75–76

play
    of exceptionally bright children, 9
    families as basis for pretend play, 76–77
    geometric concepts, exploring, 90–91
    social-emotional challenges of, 109–10
    teaching how to join, 113

portfolio documentation, 23–25

praise, value of, 55, 121

pre-assessment, 25